PARENTS OF THE HOMOSEXUAL

PARENTS
OF THE HOMOSEXUAL

by

David K. Switzer

and

Shirley Switzer

THE WESTMINSTER PRESS

Philadelphia

Scripture quotations from the Revised Standard Version
of the Bible are copyrighted 1946, 1952, © 1971, 1973
by the Division of Christian Education of the National
Council of the Churches of Christ in the U.S.A., and are
used by permission.

Book Design by Dorothy Alden Smith

First edition

Published by The Westminster Press®
Philadelphia, Pennsylvania

PRINTED IN THE UNITED STATES OF AMERICA
9 8 7 6 5 4 3 2 1

Library of Congress Cataloging in Publication Data

Switzer, David K   1925–
    Parents of the homosexual.

    (Christian care books ; 11)
    Bibliography: p.
    1. Homosexuality—Moral and religious aspects.
2. Homosexuals—Family relationships. 3. Parent
and child. 4. Parenting. I. Switzer, Shirley,
1925–   joint author. III. Series.
HQ76.25.S93   306.7'6   80–13748
ISBN 0–664–24327–4

Contents

Preface

We want to express our appreciation to Dr. Wayne E. Oates, distinguished minister, pastoral counselor, and teacher, for the opportunity which he has given us to work together with each other and with him in bringing this small book into being. We have gained from our collaboration together as husband and wife in this task and we have learned from each other. It has been good for us.

We are also grateful for the patient and supportive and helpful comments of Dr. Oates as we have moved along in the process. His commitment to the work of this series as expressed in his prompt and constructive replies to our material has been impressive.

Of course, we could not have accomplished what we have done here without the confidence expressed in us by those homosexual persons who have come to us to discuss the most serious issues of their lives, most of them in formal counseling relationships, but some just as friend to friend. The same is true for the numerous parents who have shared their anguished questioning with us. We also want to mention specifically those persons who have come forward to offer their own experiences to us when they have heard that we were writing such a book. We cherish their friendship and are indebted to them.

Finally, and once again, we are extremely grateful to Gladys Mollet—secretary par excellence, competent, and above all, good-spirited in the face of the pressures of deadlines and patient with the endless correcting and retyping. In a real sense, she, too, has written this book.

DAVID AND SHIRLEY SWITZER

Dallas, Texas

Introduction

This book is primarily for parents who suspect or have just recently discovered that their son or daughter is homosexual, and particularly for those parents whose Christian faith and participation in the church has some meaning. It is our sincere desire that what we say here will be helpful to you and to other parents in what for most families is a very disturbing and stressful situation.

We know that you must be aware that everything we describe will not necessarily coincide exactly with your reactions and needs. That can't be, since people and situations differ so radically, even where there is some core experience that is the same or at least somewhat similar. The terrain over which we will walk with you is still not completely explored. It may seem strange, confusing, and sometimes unpleasant. The book is yet to be written to which even a majority of people can say, "This is it, definitively." There are obvious reasons for divergence on the issues we will be discussing here.

First, people's experiences actually differ. Homosexual persons experience themselves differently from one another, and events differ. Parents are at quite different places emotionally and in their relationships with their children and in their knowledge of homosexuality and the gay life.

Secondly—perhaps this should have been listed first because of its tremendous influence—this is obviously a highly emotionally charged subject. It certainly is for most parents. Part of the reason is that homosexuality is an area of some combination of ignorance, prejudice, fear, and anxiety on the part of a large number of people in this and many other countries, and many of these people are parents. It is certainly not surprising that when they discover that *their own* son or daughter is homosexual these reactions are intensified. Even for people with some amount of knowledge, who are committed to the basic rights of all persons, who are "liberal" in outlook, who are basically compassionate and understanding, somehow when it is *their* son or daughter, emotionally it usually all becomes different, at least for a while.

The subject is highly charged emotionally for gay persons themselves. It is *their* lives. *They* have usually had problems adjusting to *themselves* as they are. It is often an emotional problem between them and their parents, whether the parents know or don't know. *They* have been the butt of jokes and had to keep their mouths shut. *They* have been the target of discrimination, prejudice, often direct verbal abuse, and sometimes physical attack. It is certainly an emotional area for them.

Finally, to be quite candid, even professional researchers and helping persons have yet to reach any consensus on what homosexuality is, what "causes" it, what should be done about it, what *the* biblical position on it is. Therefore they have different theories based on differing and incomplete data which have been accumulated by different procedures and drawn from different populations of homosexual persons. They make different interpretations of their observations, and therefore on the basis of their present positions, support different courses of action. They even just plain have their own personal opinions and feelings. Such differences among conscientious, honest, and competent people should give all of us cause to temper our remarks with some degree of tentativeness. One researcher may say, "This is definitely what I have discovered." And it is. But that doesn't necessarily mean that it covers all cases. One homosexual person may say, "I know that *this* is the reason I'm gay, and this is the way my life is for me." And that may be so, but other gay persons may have experiences that are different from that. One parent may say, "This is what it's like in *our* family," but this doesn't describe other families. One biblical scholar says the word means this and another scholar says it means that, or they come to different conclusions using what seems to be the same information. Overall, it is a complex and even confusing picture. However, there *is* information, and it can be put together to form clearer pictures than that which perhaps we have had up until this time. The task of putting differing material together is what we set out to do here.

But why? We are writing this book mainly out of our deep concern for parents and their sons and daughters who are in this difficult and agonizing time within themselves and with one another, and we do so mainly out of our experiences with young people and adults who are homosexual and with their parents. We trust that this work will help you better understand yourselves and your son or daughter, and that you will gain some guidance and support in what is for most parents in this situation a time of real stress, conflict, and self-examination. We hope that it will play some role in the movement toward genuine reconciliation and mutual love and respect in your family.

We realize that what we describe here may not coincide exactly with your reactions and needs, and also that we may interpret the Bible differently from the way you do and may come to conclusions that are different from yours. While we naturally think we have good reasons for interpreting the Scripture as we do (which you will read in Chapter 9) and for reaching our conclusions on what homosexuality is and on what the Bible says about it, it is our experience that equally sincere Christians and conscientious persons do not always believe the same things. While all of us are basically united in faith we have a variety of perspectives. It is in the sharing of these with one another that we learn and grow and are strengthened in our life and faith. We may or may not agree that the Bible speaks only of homosexual *acts* and not of the *condition* of homosexuality, that all homosexual acts are morally wrong and sinful or that only some are, that homosexuality is a condition of some persons from the earliest stages of their lives and that they have no choice about their sexual orientation or that it may at least sometimes be a matter of learning in which there is also some decision and responsibility.

Regardless of what you believe about these issues, you need to realize that your positions on them must not be allowed to interfere with your dealing effectively with the confusion and emotional distress which you as parents are probably undergoing, with the stress that is usually placed on the relationship between yourselves, and with your need to understand and have a good relationship with your son or daughter. We are convinced that regardless of a person's position on these issues, the essential tasks that we outline in this book are necessary to accomplish and can be accomplished.

Having made a concerted effort to look at many books on homosexuality, yet well aware that there are many we have not yet seen, at this point we have found only two that were specifically written for parents (Betty Fairchild and Nancy Hayward, *Now That You Know: What Every Parent Should Know About Homosexuality;* Harcourt Brace Jovanovich, 1979; and Charles Silverstein, *A Family Matter: A Parent's Guide to Homosexuality;* McGraw-Hill Book Co., 1977). Each of these books has genuine value. Whereas Silverstein takes into consideration a person's religious background and participation and shows a respectful attitude toward what is meaningful to this person, he does not explicitly deal with religious issues. Fairchild and Hayward do have a good chapter on this topic, but their book does not seem to be *primarily* directed toward people in the church.

Therefore we write specifically with church people in mind. If, however, you have gotten hold of this book and read to this point, but do not have any religious affiliation or any particular religious concerns, don't stop yet. In the first place, we don't believe that on the basis of religion alone there are essential differences of emotional reaction to the discovery that one's son or daughter is or may be homosexual. Secondly, we don't believe that our explicit references to the resources of faith and the biblical material will stand in the way of your receiving some important insights and perhaps emotional support.

Even though the book is particularly for parents, we certainly hope that gay persons will read it to provide themselves with the groundwork for a better understanding of what their parents are going through now that they know about their children's sexual orientation. Unexpected reactions of parents (such as not much reaction at all at first but then later a great deal of hurt and anger), behavior that may be extreme (*great* anger, threats, blame), or behavior that may be even more uncomfortable than these just mentioned (abject self-blame, uncontrollable weeping, depression), may all be understood as normal, given *their* situation and perspective, and as transient, especially if both the gay persons and their parents are dedicated to "hanging in there" for a period of time as they continue to communicate with one another.

Who are we to dare to write a book like this? Especially when a book discusses a situation that is as problematic as homosexuality in the family, it may be important to a number of readers to know something of our experience and perspective. Shirley is a Master's level psychologist who worked in a public mental health clinic before going into private practice. She has worked with numerous homosexual persons on a number of issues in their lives and with quite a few homosexual couples on problems of their living together, like the problems of many people in their marriage and family life. In this work she has had occasion to meet and discuss with some of these clients' parents their own feelings, their attempts to understand their children, and their difficulties in the process of developing a good and new relationship within the family. David is a minister, having served local churches, been a college chaplain, for several years a counselor to students and their families at a theological seminary, a part-time psychiatric hospital chaplain at the same time, and now a full-time teacher in the field of pastoral care and counseling at that school. In all these settings he has known homosexual persons and sometimes their parents. He has talked with the young persons about their relationship with their parents and vice versa. We are also parents ourselves and know something of what it is to love deeply our own children; to have and to let go, to experience conflict, to suffer with, and to value a continuing relationship with them now that they are grown and married.

Coming as they do out of our own experience, the events and conversations referred to are those of real persons in anguish and conflict, struggling to understand, trying to make sense out of their situation, to reach a point of resolution. Much of what is reported here is with the knowledge and permission of those involved, but even in these instances and certainly in the others a variety of factors such as location, sex, and specific details of other kinds in the situations described have been de-identified or changed or made into a composite picture. Some of these persons would not mind at all being identified and have said so. Others, of course, are not ready for this, and we respect where they are at this time.

1. "Oh, No!"

"He came into the kitchen while his father and I were having a cup of coffee. He looked so serious that we stopped our conversation and I asked him if anything was wrong. He didn't answer, just got a cup of coffee for himself, and sat down at the table with us. He took a long time to stir in the sugar and cream and didn't look at me even once. Finally, he said, 'I want to tell you something and it's the hardest thing I've ever had to do.' I felt my stomach begin to knot up and noticed that my son's face seemed drawn and pale. I glanced at my husband and he was just staring grimly down into his cup. We all seemed frozen in place for a minute, and then our son blurted out, 'I'm gay!' I couldn't believe it. I felt dizzy and sick, and my child seemed an absolute stranger. I thought, Oh, no! Not *my* son, not that bright, dear little child that I had read to, tucked into bed, who had been grandparents' favorite and teacher's pet. There had been some ghastly mistake."

"Oh, no!"

We all have said these words. They are the very natural, immediate, spontaneous response of any human being to some event or to the report of some event or to some other information that is first experienced as being unbelievable or emotionally intolerable to us.

"Did you hear that Joe had a heart attack?"

Or, ". . . that Mary's son was killed in an automobile accident?"

Or, ". . . that Sue is an alcoholic?"

Or, "I hate to break this news to you, but the tests show that you have cancer."

Or,— Add your own experience: your family, your friends.

"Oh, no!" We don't even think about the words. They force themselves out instantaneously as the genuine expression of our denial that this is so, of our desire that it *not* be so.

"Mom, Dad, I have something to tell you. I'm gay."

"Oh, no!"

The words of the mother in the above incident are fairly typical. "You *can't* be. Why, you are *our* child. You must be wrong. This must be a sick joke. Don't tell me. Don't talk about it."

At some level, these words represent the internal response that parents have to a thought and a group of feelings which they feel they cannot bear. Everything in them combines to reject it. Few events are more painful to parents than getting the news that their son or daughter either has been forced in some way or another or has chosen a course in life that is counter to a value system which they hold dear and/or to the expectations, whether conscious or unconscious, spoken or unspoken, that all of us parents have for our children.

This is especially true when sons or daughters announce to their parents that they are homosexual, or when parents hear this word from someone else. Even for parents who have suspected for a period of time that this might be the case, and many have, it still comes as a shock. For some parents, homosexuality is seen to be desperately, desperately wrong morally. It is radically out of kilter with the way things are supposed to be; it is "unnatural," "against nature," "sick." Even among parents who view themselves as being enlightened, who have an intellectual understanding of what homosexuality is which allows them to be tolerant if not accepting of people who are homosexual, when it is *their* child it is different. Something deeply buried emotionally rises to the surface and rejects this reality.

Shock and denial have been clearly identified and their role in our lives investigated in connection with a number of other major life crises. Among them are two very common ones. Dr. Elisabeth Kübler-Ross, in her book *On Death and Dying* (Macmillan Co., 1969), reports the results of her interviews with over two hundred terminally ill patients. She states that the first reaction to the discovery of their illness on the part of almost all of them was denial: "No, not me; it cannot be true." There is a combination of the intellectual rejection of the fact and emotional numbness, the experience of "no feeling at all." This reaction is as natural a response by the person's mind and emotions to overwhelmingly painful reality as that of the body's shock to severe physical trauma. It is a buffer, a temporary protection against the pain, allowing the person some time to mobilize other defenses and resources with which to deal with the distress. It serves the purpose of allowing the impact of the reality to filter through into the conscious mind in smaller amounts. Gradually, then, by bits and pieces, the whole truth can be assimilated, and, in varying degrees, accepted.

The same initial experience is observed in grief, and all authorities list shock, numbness, denial as the first stage. Dr. C. Murray Parkes, a British research psychiatrist, in his book, *Bereavement: Studies of Grief in Adult Life* (International Universities Press, 1972), speaks of the "blunting" of the emotions that comes on very quickly after a person with whom we are closely related emotionally has died. This emotional blunting, he has discovered, lasts from a few hours to a few days, although sometimes it may last even longer. He reports an interview with one woman who found her husband's body on the stairs. The first stab of pain expressed itself with loud and long wails. But within a few minutes she began to feel numb all over. "I felt numb and solid for a week. It's a blessing." She realized that the numbness that kept the pain away enabled her to cope with her children during that time, to make arrangements for the funeral, and to deal with the details of the gathering family. Yet, along with the numbness for many persons is the underlying sense of impending disaster.

Numerous parents have reported that their reaction to the knowledge that their child was homosexual was like losing the child. It was as if the child had died. Some have even said that it felt worse than a death to them because of the many complicating feelings, because they share the larger society's abhorrence of the very thought of homosexual feelings and behavior. The denial and shock that is reported as the first stage of one's knowledge of a terminal illness and of grief is also usually the first stage of the reaction to hearing about a child's homosexuality. "Oh, no! It can't be true. Not *our* child." During the first hours and days following such a discovery, some parents report a sense of unreality about it all, just as a person in grief will. A parent will catch himself or herself looking out of the corner of the eye at the son or daughter, and there is a shudder, and then the unreal feeling that it is all a terrible dream. It *cannot* be so. The parents expect any minute to hear the words, "It's all been a mistake." But for the majority, the words do not come.

We parents have typically invested so much of ourselves in our children that much of the pain and disorder of their experience or of their misbehavior produces pain in us also. This is natural. Even beyond this, though, there are some parents whose own sense of identity has been so shaky as individuals that they have now begun to find their identity only as parents of their children or of a particular child. They are seeking to live out their own lives through the lives of their children. For these parents, any disappointment or disillusionment in their children is a particularly severe blow to them. It is a severe threat to the meaning of their own lives.

Accompanying our investments in our children are our expectations of them. Most of us would prefer to say that we really have none. We only want them to be healthy and happy. But also for most of us, whether we admit it or not, we rather naturally have our own images of what our children's happiness looks like. We may not require that they finish high school or go to college, but it has never occurred to us that they won't. We may not put external pressure on them to take over the family business or follow the father into his job. In fact, we may well criticize some other parents for doing this. But if the child is *too* different (the boy wants to be an artist or dancer or interior designer, or the girl wants to be a doctor or a construction worker), we discover that something emotional in us resists the child's desire, and we find very logical reasons to try to get across to the child why he or she should not do this.

Among the usually unspoken expectations that we have is that our children will be heterosexual, will marry, and will have children. This is usually unspoken (at least until about ages twenty-two to twenty-four or so, depending upon our own particular subculture and family tradition), because it never even occurs to most of us to question that this is what is going to happen. It is so deeply engrained within us that heterosexuality, marriage, and children is the way it is and will be. Every aspect of this wishful expectation is destroyed by the revelation, however it comes to parents, that their son or daughter is homosexual.

Most teenagers and young adults who suspect or think or know that they are homosexual are extremely reluctant to tell their parents directly about it. Some are ashamed. They themselves are confused and don't understand it and often have the same feelings about themselves that they expect other persons to have. Some are terrified as they imagine their parents' reactions. Some withhold because they are angry with their parents. Some don't tell because they genuinely don't want to hurt other family members. But the pressures created by maintaining a facade over the years begin to take their toll, and sooner or later the teenager or young adult realizes that this reality may need to be shared with the rest of the family. It is an awful moment, as much for the homosexual person as for the parents themselves.

Often the young persons or young adults will reveal the information about their homosexuality in a serial fashion over a period of time. They will drop different clues, hoping that someone else will initiate the conversation that will lead ultimately to the revelation. Also often enough, they will test the information first on a brother or sister who has been a trusted friend with the hope that this person's reaction will encourage them to move on to a parent or both parents. Or, they may hope that the brother or sister will tell the parents for them. If their relationship with their brother or sister has been good, if there have been many shared experiences, it is likely that the first response will not entail so much shock, because there is not the same kind or amount of emotional investment between siblings as there is between parents and their children. The revelation to a brother or sister can serve as a bellwether or signal concerning parental "readiness" and in addition provide a buffer and support when the time comes to inform the parents.

A young man shares his experience: "I hinted around for weeks to my sister and finally just took my friend who was also my lover over to her house for dinner. I introduced him to her and she said: 'My brother has told me so much about you. I almost feel like I'm meeting his fiancée.' Then she really blushed and we all started laughing like crazy. I remember that I also felt like crying. When we finally calmed down, I said, 'You knew all along, didn't you?' She said: 'You mean that you and Jim are more than roommates? Yeah,

I figured you guys were gay a long time ago, and you know what? It's okay with me.' Then I did cry some and hugged her and told her I sure wished she had told me a long time ago. It was like a lot of tension went out of my body. Now the big job is mom and dad."

In this case the young man went on to tell his parents. Even though they had suspected for some time that he was homosexual, the clear announcement of it was still a shock. The mother cried and the father was grim. It was a difficult situation, but the sense of the sister's support had helped him do what was important to him.

A young woman tells of a quite different initial reaction: "I told my sister I was in love with a woman and she said that I couldn't be because I was married and had a kid. I told her I was getting a divorce and moving in with my lover and that we were going to raise my daughter. She told me that I was crazy and she didn't want to hear any more and that I sure hadn't better tell my folks because it would kill my father. I felt bad a long time after that because my sister and I had been really close and never did have any secrets from each other. But that's turned out okay. We're cool with each other now."

After beginning to work things out with her sister, she went on to tell her mother. The mother, like the sister, was stunned and hurt. But in the midst of the pain, she too responded: "Your father must never know. It would just kill him." Poor father, protected from the real world by all the women in his life.

"But we are Christians. We've been active in the church. Our son has grown up in the church. He knows what the Bible says about homosexuality." The outcry, "How then could this possibly happen to us?" is natural and understandable as a cry of anguish. The Bible has many comparable spontaneous outbursts of pain and confusion. "If we're God's chosen people, why are we allowed to suffer, to be defeated, et cetera?"

But the Bible itself also makes it clear that no protection is promised against the many possible threats that life has inherent within it: sickness, pain, death, distress of many kinds. To be sure, there are references to God as a rock, a shield and buckler, a very present help in trouble, and many other expressions to reinforce the experience that God is a present strength and support, and that, no matter what the immediate circumstances, God will also be with us in the future. But the same realities of life are the common experience of all humanity. "He sends rain on the just and on the unjust."

Some children do grow up in Sunday school and church, in Christian homes, and somewhere along the line realize that they have sexual feelings for another person of the same sex. Parents who are active members of the church have then experienced the shock, followed by the anguish and mental and emotional confusion, that overcomes them upon the discovery that their child is homosexual.

The purpose of this book is to try to help you, if you suspect or have found out by whatever means that your child is homosexual. It is an attempt to assist you in dealing with what is going on in your situation by discussing some of the major typical questions and thoughts and feelings that others have had in the same circumstances: the denial, the grief, the blaming of others and oneself, the anger, the shame, the confusion. If you have some or all of these feelings, you are normal. More often than not, they are to be expected.

We also hope to give you in brief summary the best information that we can come up with in regard to what homosexuality is, what the meaning of the Bible may be to you and your family in this situation, how your own thinking and feeling may begin to change, and how healing and reconciliation may begin to take place in the family.

Reconciliation can come. It does not *always,* but it may: if the young person is candid and kindness is mutual; if the young person can understand and be patient with the rather understandable first negative reaction that most parents have; if the young person does not take as the final word any of the many things parents may say out of their own new and strong feelings and confusion; if parents can be more understanding of their own initial reactions so they may then give primary attention to trying to understand their child through many long conversations; if the parents can give themselves and their children the time to allow the love that may really be there between them to rise to the surface and become the most influential of the variety of feelings present.

This chapter opened with the story of a young man who told his parents that he was gay. Their initial reaction was shock and denial. "Oh, no!" It was an intolerable thought and the feelings were painful. For a while the parents simply put the information away. They refused to talk about it with each other. But time went on and with its passing came understanding and healing. This process was aided by the willingness and courage of parents and son alike to accept the possibility that there could be a relationship beyond the pain and disagreement. In this family the son is now accepted as he is. His parents are proud of his work in his chosen profession and thoroughly enjoy his company. This is a goal worth working for.

2. "We've Lost Our Child"

"When my son finally was able to get across to me that he was gay, it was like being told that he was dead. Suddenly the person sitting across from me wasn't my son anymore. I felt as if I were talking with a stranger."

This father was describing the powerful experience he had when in the midst of talking with his son, the information that this young man in his late twenties was homosexual suddenly came through to him and transformed the scene. A stranger was telling this man that his son had died. The stranger looked like his son. The voice was the same. But the son as the father had known him was dead.

The father discovered that he could not look his son directly in the eyes; he couldn't touch him; he couldn't embrace him. He felt dead inside himself. He felt empty. It was only after many months of tension and pain, and after a minister talked with both of them and helped them express their confusion, disappointment, anger, love, and their desire to work for a better relationship, that the father was able to put his arms around his son and hold him.

Another young man was telling of the reaction of his father. They lived in different parts of the country, so the son wrote his parents that he was gay and was "coming out," that is, beginning to live openly as a homosexual. Then when they talked next on the phone, the father exclaimed in a rage: "It's a good thing you're not around here. I'd kill you." After a pause in the account, one of the authors of this book said to the young man: "I imagine you can probably understand your father's tremendous anger toward you. After all, you killed his son." The young man responded with genuine realization of what that statement meant: "Yeah! Yeah, I guess I did."

In Chapter 1 we spoke of the initial sense of shock and the natural tendency to deny the reality of what we are being told. We compared this reaction with that which people have in crises in which they experience reality as being so painful or frightening or angering as to be utterly intolerable. It is, as we mentioned, also the first stage in grief.

It is very common for parents initially to experience the fact of their son's or daughter's homosexuality as if that person had died. Rationally everyone can tell that it is not *objectively* a loss. The person is right there: alive, talking, usually wanting to be the child of his or her parents. But at another level, it is inevitable that many parents, in varying degrees of course, experience the revelation as a death: the loss of the valued person whom they thought and felt they had, the loss of a dream, of an illusion.

We parents invest so much in our children. At first they are totally, absolutely dependent upon us for physical, emotional, and spiritual sustenance. They are dependent upon us for the learning of behavior that will help them survive, grow, enjoy relationships, become competent. We can see over the years the ways in which they learn what we consciously and unconsciously teach them. We love them, and we are quite aware of their responsiveness to us, even when some of that responsiveness is anger when they are frustrated. We invest ourselves in them. It is difficult for us to think of our future without continuing relationship with them, and their future involves us. In a very real sense, our own being is tied up with them and theirs with us. We experience them as extensions of ourselves. They literally become a part of us.

All of this, as we hope we are making clear, is unavoidable, given the totally helpless state of the newborn. Yet we are well aware that the task of good parenting is to assist our children through the years to become more and more their own persons, less dependent upon us, more autonomous. We try to live with them and teach them so they develop a value system that is genuinely their own, values that operate within their lives apart from us. We hope they will have a faith that is vital and personal and not just a collection of thoughts and practices inherited from us. Many times, both for children and parents, this process of their becoming less dependent and more autonomous is a wrenching, agonizing one, as the pulling apart hurts. The growing separateness may at times feel like rejection or alienation. Considering the mutual investments in one another, the identifications with one another, we begin to understand that when a child or a parent dies, we experience not only a loss of someone "out there" but also a loss of a part of ourselves. We feel dead, or empty. We experience the terrible pain of a vital part of our own being as it is torn out of our own "insides."

But death, as we all know, is not the only form of loss, and there are many ways in which parents have felt the loss of a child which is not physical death. For many parents, the discovery that their son or daughter is homosexual is experienced as a loss of the *child* because it *is* a loss of so many of the elements that have ordinarily made up the relationship between the parent and the child: our *interpretation* of who our child is, which, with most parents, has never included even the possibility that the child would be anything but heterosexual; the dreams and expectations of whom they would become (married, "respectable" members of the community and the church, having children of their own, which obviously includes our dreams about whom *we* will become, namely, grandparents to their children). We have assumed they would continue pretty much the life-style that our family has had, accept our value system, always be a part of "our group" (and by implication not be a part of a group of which "we" don't approve). To the extent that we have actually seen parts of ourselves in our children as they have grown up, it now feels as if these are being rejected by them, as if we are no longer their parents and they no longer our children.

Silverstein recounts in detail the story of Amy Peterson after her daughter told her mother that she was gay. There were different reactions during the day: first, very little at all, but later the feeling of being sick. "That night Amy Peterson had a nightmare. She was standing in front of a pair of large doors, with a big keyhole in them. A man came over with the keys and opened the doors. He pushed them wide apart. They opened upon a big gymnasium, brightly illuminated with floodlights. In the center of the gym was a row of long tables, and on each table there were four small black caskets. The top of each casket was open, and they all contained dead infants. Around the tables were men and women dressed in black. They were parents mourning for their children, the women beating their breasts. She noticed one woman in particular who was wailing over her dead child. Amy walked toward the woman. She stood by the table and saw that the wailing woman was herself, and the dead infant was Susan. Amy awoke, shaking, and realized that she was coming to think of her daughter as dead." (Silverstein, *A Family Matter*, pp. 32–33.)

We don't want to overstate this point, because this description does not fit all parents with the same degree of intensity. However, it is our observation that most parents, when they first discover that their son or daughter is homosexual, have some aspects of this reaction that they have lost their child. In this sense, parents experience grief, with all of its complexities. If this is a valid comparison, then it means that the parents' response to this new knowledge is not going to be satisfactorily dealt with in just a few hours or days, nor is it just going to go away automatically with the passing of time. Grief is a process with several identifiable stages. It takes some amount of time to go through. A number of things are necessary or important to assist persons in going through these stages constructively. To understand the sense of loss of or estrangement from one's child as being like grief can be very helpful to a parent in a number of ways.

1. You are going through a process that is not just peculiar to you and to you in this set of circumstances, but is shared by most persons at one time or another.

2. Your first reactions will probably not persist with the same strength that they now have. They will tend to diminish.

3. The intensity of feelings, the conflicts, and confusion, and the behavior that results, are not abnormal, unless the behaviors become extreme or unless the feelings and behavior persist unabated after six or eight months to a year.

4. It will probably take quite some time for you to adjust to your feelings and thoughts about yourselves and your child, so you need to be tolerant of yourselves and explain to your child his or her need to be tolerant of you during this process.

5. You need to be aware of, accept, and talk frequently about your feelings and confusion, even if this becomes repetitive.

6. The sharing of all of this openly within the family is very important. You need to let every other family member know where you are with your thoughts and feelings at any given time.

7. The support of understanding and trusted persons outside the family (friends, minister) can be helpful in diminishing the intensity of your feelings and renewing your self-esteem.

8. As in death, this event is a challenge to faith. Some people

become angry with God and question God, some reject God, but many find that a deep trust in the compassionate, forgiving, sustaining God is in fact redeeming.

Our purpose here is to assist you to understand more clearly what is going on within you, what you might expect to experience, and therefore to help you feel somewhat better about yourself and to deal more constructively with yourself as a person, with your spouse, and with your child. In order to accomplish these goals, let us look in more detail at the stages of grief. These are based on the research of Dr. C. Murray Parkes, who was referred to in Chapter 1.

We have already stated that the first stage is *shock and denial.* Certainly we all can understand this, and all of us have experienced shock in other instances. Denial takes numerous forms, but none is so clear as what may stand as a classic response on the part of one mother when her daughter told her that she was gay. "Oh no you're not," the mother answered immediately and went right on with the conversation on an entirely different subject, as if the daughter had said nothing more startling than, "It's going to rain today." This daughter was twenty-five years old at the time.

One young man had the following impression of his parents' reaction when he first told them. "It was as if they were beyond emotion. It was like a scene in which they'd just received a message that their son was dead, and they seemed to be treating me like the man who delivered the telegram. Mother began to weep. They expressed disappointment, but after a while they just weren't able to talk any longer."

Parents in this situation of first discovery often report a sense of unreality, as if this scene were just a dream. Or they themselves feel unreal or as if the whole world about them is unreal. This is a part of shock, and is not to be feared. It is a normal reaction.

Of course, other feelings may be a part of the initial reaction to the extent that shock and denial are not complete, as they often are not. Among responses that persons report are feeling sick at their stomachs or feeling sick all over, a sense of impending disaster, as if one's world is crumbling, a stabbing pain, anguish, trembling, feeling faint, or perhaps great anger. The first stage may last only a few hours or days, although often longer if parents are able to maintain their denial. It is certainly natural to want to maintain the belief that what they have heard is not so.

The second stage of grief comes with the diminishing of shock and as the reality of the son's or daughter's life as it has now been described to us is reinforced in a number of ways. Parkes calls this stage *yearning*. It includes a variety of strong and often conflicting feelings and those behaviors which seek, in the case of death, to keep the person alive, to find the person, or in some instances to join the person where he or she is. In the awareness of your child's homosexuality, as in death, there will be pain, anguish, anger, guilt, confusion, feeling dead or empty inside, sadness, and often revulsion, nausea, weeping, sleeplessness, not wanting to eat, difficulty in acting in your former natural and spontaneous ways with your son or daughter, such as the withdrawal of the physical expressions of your love as we mentioned earlier. In the midst of all of this may be new and disturbing thoughts. One father began to worry that his homosexual son was going to kill himself. He then became preoccupied with his wife's health, how his son's declaration of his sexuality was affecting her adversely, and often stating this effect in exaggerated terms. Some parents even have suicidal feelings triggered within themselves.

Many behaviors are directed toward keeping things the way they used to be, or at least the way the parents thought they were and wanted them to be. Parents rush in with suggestions, from thinly veiled to overt coercion, bribery, or earnest and open discussion as attempts to "fix it" somehow. "You must see a psychiatrist." "Have you prayed about it? If you would only start going to church and truly accept Christ." Parents may play on a child's sympathy or sense of loyalty to the family, or may threaten withdrawal of financial support.

All of this may sound harsh and hard on parents. It is not meant to be. First, it *is* reporting actual and somewhat frequent behavior. Second, it is understandable as being among the *early* reactions. You *do* want to try to fix it, to get your son or daughter *changed* and be heterosexual, marry, have children. Parents' lives have been radically altered in their present experience, so they are often angry and they often feel panic.

Parents may spend a lot of time daydreaming about when their child was younger, looking at pictures or toys or clothing or awards that remind them of earlier and happier days before their dreams were shattered.

Parkes's third stage of grief is *disorganization and despair.* His description of it in regard to the response to death has its similarities here too. It begins with the diminishing of the intensity of the feelings and the behaviors of stage two. Weeping, anger, guilt, confusion, grow less. The child may make some efforts to please the parents by going to a counselor or attending church, but more often than not this fails to accomplish what the parents want. The truth of the child's homosexuality gradually sinks in and is accepted as the way it is going to be. An uneasy truce may be made with the child. But there is still unhappiness, tension within the parents, often between the parents, and between them and their son or daughter. Most of the attempts to recapture the past are given up, but the central task of developing their future as persons and as a family in the light of the new reality has not yet been accomplished. The future is not thought about much, and when it is, it seems dark and dreary.

The final stage is *reorganization.* The attempts to hold on to the past and to the last vestiges of hope that the homosexual son or daughter will miraculously change disappear and the situation is seen for what it truly is. Genuine reconciliation may begin to take place as relationships between the parents and between them and their son or daughter begin to improve. Even though the parents do not necessarily approve of the child's behavior, the child is loved and accepted. The parents can look to their own future with their self-images revised but with self-esteem instead of self-blame and self-pity. Anger has been expressed and worked through; sadness is lessened, although it may persist and be felt from time to time; any depression that parents have felt over this situation is gone. Just as the parents' reactions in the other stages described here must not be interpreted as being too "bad," too pessimistic, the description of this stage must not be seen as always too "good," too optimistic. All parent-child problems and all marriage problems that may have arisen during this time are not necessarily completely solved. Disappointment and some sadness may never go away. But there is a basic reorganization of individual and family life if the earlier stages of the process have been handled well.

Like the death of a family member, the information that a son or daughter is homosexual also has the initial impact of changing family members' perceptions of one another, and therefore it changes and is a threat to the family system itself. Not only do parents respond differently to that particular person, but often there is the development of tension between the parents themselves. Occasionally, the death of a child will immediately draw the husband and wife closer to each other. Many times, however, barriers arise between them. They pull away from each other as severe readjustments in their own relationship are made necessary. Needs that were formerly met by the presence of the child are obviously not met any longer. Parents look to each other to meet those needs at a time when each one of them is obviously less capable of doing so, and this produces frustration, tension, anger. Even when the parents have similar experiences, each may react differently. One may have outbursts of temper. The other may withdraw. Communication is made extremely difficult under these circumstances, so that even many of the usual, everyday decisions are more difficult to make and the ordinary conflicts difficult to resolve.

Something of the same reaction may occur in the situation we are talking about here, with a few additional complications. One parent may blame the other or they both may get into the blaming game; one may be fairly understanding of the child and the other condemnatory and angry, neither spouse then understanding or supporting the other. Older unresolved issues, such as earlier losses or marital stress, may be stirred up by the pain and anxiety and increased need of this present situation. If this happens, parents need not be surprised or dismayed. It does not necessarily mean the end of things for them. If they realize that it is fairly common that such tensions arise, this can help them to have more understanding of themselves and each other and thus be better prepared to work on the realistic differences between them at this time. Many parents discover that they need to consult someone else to help them work out these issues, and therefore they go to their minister or to a marriage counselor.

Of course, there are differences between this situation and other situations of grief. In death there is a body to help make the fact of the loss more concrete: viewing the body, having the funeral, observing the burial. In contrast, the homosexual son or daughter is still there, continuing to stimulate the many feelings and the confusion. "He looks and sounds like the child of ours whom we've known for so long; we share common memories. But this person is different, and I behave differently toward him."

At the time of death, church members and other friends and neighbors visit. They are with us as we weep and talk about our loss.

They are understanding and supportive, since death is universal. They join with us in the common language and acts of the funeral service as together we remember the one we love in the midst of our worship of God. All of this is sustaining and strengthening for us.

Discovering that a son or daughter is homosexual is seldom a public event. Other persons are not in a position to know. Usually parents do not want to tell anyone. Even when they do tell one or two trusted friends, these friends sometimes feel very ill at ease and don't know how to respond, especially at first. Others who may find out about the situation tend *not* to come and offer themselves in this time of need because of their own discomfort.

In the case of a death, people often feel more a part of a community of faith and support; in the case of the discovery that a son or daughter is homosexual, they usually feel more isolated and are left alone within their families to experience in their various ways their burden, guilt, shame, anger, disruption, confusion. In fact, one mother expressed her feelings in the following way: "I'd rather he *was* dead. If my child had died, his potential and dignity and morality would have been intact and I could have been proud. Now I am shamed with how he has turned out."

However, to see the similarities between the grief that is in reaction to death and the complex reactions to the disclosure that your son or daughter is homosexual provides a perspective for you which can help you understand more adequately the experience you are going through. It assures you that what you are experiencing within yourselves as individuals and between each other and your family is not somehow abnormal. A combination of these feelings and behaviors is to be expected. You can prepare yourselves to tolerate some of them, because after a while they will diminish and some even vanish. You can allow yourselves to feel some of the emotions deeply; in fact, you *need* to allow yourselves to feel them rather than repress them and pretend they are not there. You can push yourselves to talk openly and honestly with one another within the family as a way of resolving some of the issues. You can appreciate the fact that often enough it is helpful to talk with a minister or other professional counselor about yourselves and your situation. You are reminded that your experiences are a part of a process that must be gone all the way through, and not a situation in which you can successfully bypass important tasks and skip stages. It will take time.

Several times we will be suggesting that you discuss your situation with a minister or a mental health professional. Sometimes this will be to try to gain a perspective on your son's or daughter's homosexuality or suspected homosexuality, sometimes to discuss your own relationship with each other because of the stress so often stimulated, sometimes to seek assistance in improving your relationship with your son or daughter, sometimes to assist you in going through the stages of your own confusion and distress with its variety of feelings.

If you choose to go to a minister, you need to remember that ministers are also people. They differ from one another, and may differ from you. They believe different things about homosexuality, depending upon their interpretation of the Bible and upon their variety of feelings about this sexual orientation and behavior. It may be confusing or even frustrating to you if the minister's views on homosexuality and homosexual persons vary from yours. This is not the major issue, however. Such a minister may still be able to love you and your son or daughter, listen to you, help you clarify your own feelings, and help you communicate more effectively with one another. In this process, you can be helped significantly.

Nevertheless, if you discover that the minister is uptight emotionally about the matter, and therefore not able to listen attentively and communicate understanding, if the minister is condemnatory of homosexual persons, then the goals of emotional expression, mutual understanding, and reconciliation which you desire for yourselves and your family will probably not be achieved. If you realize this after your initial conversation, you would do well to find someone else with whom to talk. You must consider your own needs, and not the program of a minister who does not have the sensitivity to help you discover and work out your goals.

Finally, it is important to remember Paul's call in II Corinthians to all Christians to join in "the ministry of reconciliation," the central duty, yes, opportunity, of us all in all circumstances. In this situation, as at the time of death, Paul's words in Romans continue to be true, that nothing "will be able to separate us from the love of God in Christ Jesus our Lord" (Rom. 8:39). *Nothing!* God has not abandoned you, although you may feel that way, nor has God abandoned your son or daughter, although you may at first interpret in that manner. Rather, in this situation as in all situations, God continues to be present and to work with you toward fulfilling promises of a new future for you made originally in the covenant with the Jews and renewed in the event of Jesus the Christ.

3. Is Our Child *Really* Gay?

But wait a minute! Perhaps we have reacted too quickly. We have been writing as though it is a foregone conclusion that the young person or young adult *is* homosexual. Often parents respond prematurely in this same way. They hear from someone else that their child has been caught "messing around" with someone of the same sex. Or, they have noticed that the child hasn't dated in the usual sense, prefers to be with peers of the same sex, or has a "special friend" of the same sex. Or, the son or daughter confides in them a deep concern about having sexual attraction to someone of the same sex. Or, the child uses the actual words, "Mom, Dad, I'm gay," or "homosexual."

The frequent tendency of parents in most of these instances is to leap automatically into the midst of shock and denial, with the unconscious assumption that any one of these disclosures means one and the same thing. They automatically deny that it's true; they try to gloss it over; they don't want to talk about it. They have some of the feelings that we mentioned in Chapter 2, when all the while they may be misjudging the true nature of the situation. They may be going through all of this unnecessarily and may say things they later regret, or at the very least they fail to get the information that is necessary in order

37

for them to know more clearly what is actually going on in the life of their son or daughter and what he or she is trying to communicate to them. They miss their opportunity to be as helpful to their child as they might be.

The point is, the young person *may* be homosexual, or may *not* be. People mean different things by the word "gay" or "homosexual." The fact that persons use it about themselves does not necessarily mean that they are giving a technically accurate description of their condition. Also, the same or similar feelings or behavior in different persons of different ages may be related to different things going on in their lives. All of this needs to be explored and not reacted to prematurely with denial, panic, anger, condemnation. It is important for parents to avoid certain extremes of reaction: on the one hand, the failure to take seriously feelings or behavior which are genuinely disturbing to the young person, and on the other, the overreaction of taking too seriously that which may not be particularly troubling to the young person or which is not necessarily evidence that the person is really homosexual.

One of the authors of this book remembers the poignancy with which a young man in his late twenties spoke of his parents' casual disregard when in his middle teens he told them of his sexual feelings toward other boys. Having grown up in his home, his church, his society, he had inevitably made the same assumptions about his own sexuality that others had made, that is, that he would be heterosexual, marry, have children, and had assimilated some of the same negative feelings toward homosexuality that the people around him had. Now his own self-image was being shaken and he felt deeply worried and very bad about himself. His mother responded to his painful opening of himself with: "Oh, it's just a phase. Don't worry about it. You'll get over it." Rather than being relieved, he felt as if he were not being taken seriously. It felt like a rejection of who he was. It was making light of his agonizing struggle. Many feelings and some homosexual behavior after that, he finally found his way to a psychiatrist's office: the wrong person for him, and too late. He has had to go through years of dealing with his bad feelings about himself and his difficult efforts to work out his identity for the most part alone, certainly without his parents' or sensitive and competent professional aid. He is homosexual today, and now feels good about himself. But it was a long and painful and lonely journey. Parents can be more helpful to their children than this. They need not have the lost years of relationship.

On the other hand, some parents have treated their fourteen-year-old children who have reported homosexual feelings or an instance or two of mutual masturbation with a peer as if these early teenagers were adults who had been homosexually promiscuous. These parents' emotional and behavioral overreaction has confused the children, has had the effect of either creating or reinforcing their bad feelings about themselves, and has cut off a close and truly helpful relationship between parents and children.

What do parents need to know, and what can they do?

First, what is homosexuality anyway? Our purpose at this point is merely to attempt to give a definition. In Chapter 8 we shall say much more about the nature of the condition and the different theories as to the causes of such feelings and behavior. Now let's just take a look at some of the definitions that have been proposed.

The pamphlet put out by the Sex Information and Education Council of the U.S. (*Homosexuality;* SIECUS, 72 Fifth Avenue, New York, N. Y. 10011) states: "Homosexuality refers to emotional attachments involving sexual attraction and/or overt sexual relations between individuals—male or female—of the same sex." Very simple. But does that mean then that any person of any age who at any time has sexual feelings toward someone of the same sex or who has sexual relations with a person of the same sex *is a homosex-*

ual, is gay? No. Not so simple then. The definition enables us to say what homosexual feelings and homosexual behavior are. It does not define who *is* homosexual or gay. Human beings and our life together are far more complex than that.

The Public Affairs Pamphlet dealing with this subject (*Changing Views of Homosexuality,* #563; Public Affairs Committee, 381 Park Avenue, South, New York, N.Y. 10016) says, "Homosexuality means sexual attraction to persons of the same sex as oneself, whether male or female," which is essentially the same definition as the one above, but the second paragraph seems to sharpen this statement considerably by saying that the term refers "to persons who are exclusively or primarily attracted to members of their own sex, and who enter into sexual and affectional relations with them." This latter statement is more helpful because it doesn't label people who have occasional homosexual feelings as *being* homosexual, because they are not necessarily. It seems to allow for temporary situational forces that lead to such feelings and/or behavior. It also makes a very important distinction between feelings and behavior. However, this definition does not account for the different ages of persons and their stages of development.

A variation of this last definition is given in Lawrence J. Hatterer, *Changing Homosexuality in the Male* (McGraw-Hill Book Co., 1970), quoting Evelyn Hooker: "The term 'homosexual' when used as a noun, refers to persons who identify themselves as such and whose patterns of sexual desires and overt behavior are predominantly or exclusively directed to members of their own gender" (p. 10). A few pages later, quoting Judd Marmor, he adds the clarifying words "in adult life" (p. 17) and goes on to allow for the fact that an *adult* might be truly homosexual, but for some reason does *not* actually engage in overt homosexual behavior (such as a celibate priest, or for other religious or practical reasons, or a homosexual who is married to a person of the other sex and who is faithful to his or her spouse).

This definition and others very much like it allow for the reality of the complexity of factors which go into determining the choice of sexual objects, and the human being has the capacity for quite a variety of these. Different ways in which children are raised, different environmental situations, and other factors lead early and middle adolescents especially (eleven or twelve to fifteen or sixteen years of age) and sometimes older adolescents and even adults either to experiment with different sexual objects or even to choose a person of the opposite sex exclusively or predominately for a brief period of time. For an early or middle teenager to have sexual feelings for someone of the same sex does not necessarily mean that this person *is* a homosexual or is destined to become one in the future. For an early or middle adolescent to engage in sexual acts occasionally, or even frequently for a limited period of time, with someone of the same sex does not necessarily mean that this person *is* a homosexual or is destined to become one in the future. It *may* mean that with a given person, but often it does not. These feelings and, even on occasions, behavior in a person who is older, do not *necessarily* mean that this person *is* a homosexual. Many persons at a certain time in their lives, or even from time to time throughout their lives, may be sexually aroused by a person of the same sex, but their predominant feelings and exclusive or primary sexual expression are heterosexual.

In addition, there is a condition that is termed pseudohomosexuality. While the definition of this term, too, does not have universal agreement among experts, most do agree that these persons have homosexual feelings, think of themselves as gay, and usually label themselves as gay. Nevertheless, many (or most or all, depending upon the particular expert) do not actually engage in overt homosexual behavior and the reasons for their feelings and self-labeling are different from those of the true homosexual.

These distinctions which we have gone to some pains to detail here are important, because similar feelings, similar behaviors, and similar words on the part of different children of different ages and in different situations discussing themselves with their parents may mean very different things and need to be responded to differently.

What are some helpful ways to respond?

First and foremost, don't dodge the issue. The subject may come up in a number of ways. For the most part in this book so far, we have tended to assume that the young person or young adult has probably dropped clues from time to time, which possibly were heard and understood by the parent, or possibly were not, but finally has told the parent in some reasonably direct way with some constructive intent in mind. This is often the case.

In some instances, however, the concrete words will come out as an expression of real hostility in the midst of an argument. Numerous gay persons report that often they have been on the verge of doing just this and they have had to bite their tongues to keep from it. Sometimes biting the tongue doesn't work and they say it. It sounds harsh. "You're still trying to run my life. You've always done it, and look what kind of job you did. You've produced a queer!" "You think you're so good and know it all. What would you think if you knew I was gay?"

In other instances, parents hear from someone else: parents of a friend of the son or daughter, or unfortunately sometimes a school principal, a college dean, or even the police.

Under any circumstances the feelings of the parents are stirred up, the feelings we have already talked about. But in an argument or a call from someone else, they are worse. Regardless, the basic task is still the same: to talk about it in detail. In the case of an argument, the immediate anger has to be dealt with as in any argument before the substance of the matter can be dealt with. But then the parent, if the son or daughter has not already done so, has to go on to say, "Let's talk specifically about what you said about your being gay." Or if the parents hear from someone else, it is imperative that they initiate the conversation with their child: "I just talked to . . . , and he said that you were homosexual. That was a terrible shock to me. What about it? Tell me honestly about yourself." Even in shocking and emotional circumstances, there is the potential for serious discussion with one another and it is essential that it be done.

Please don't misunderstand. We are not trying to suggest that you can always be calm, cool, and collected. We are not saying, "Don't *feel* anything; just talk rationally." No one can advise concerning another person's feelings. Almost all parents are going to have some combination of the feelings that we have already described. If you have strong feelings, and you probably have or will, accept them for what they are. Express them in some way verbally. Tell your son or daughter how you feel. Weep if you feel like it. You can't immediately control *what* feelings arise. But your behavior can be reasonably well under control. Even though you may tremble, cry some, feel very angry, or whatever, you can still carry on the conversation (or more likely, the series of conversations) that is necessary.

To begin with, remember that your child is having some strong feelings, too. Even when the words come out in anger, your child usually cares very deeply how you react and has some fear about your response. Your child has usually thought about telling you for months or even years, mentally reviewed, planned it, and then postponed because of great anxiety.

So now that you are talking about it, however unpleasant it is for you, you need to stay with it. First of all, listen. Invite your child to tell. Then listen. The first task is absolutely necessary: to try to understand the experience of your child. This is not the same thing as immediately "approving," or agreeing, but merely understanding the past and present experiences of this person.

Ask questions that can help you understand. Make summarizing statements which either communicate that you *are* understanding, or perhaps that you are not and that you need more clarity.

Help your son or daughter review the history of his or her experiences. "When and how did you first become aware of these feelings? What was it like for you? Has it always been clear to you, or have there been times of confusion and conflicts? What feelings have you had about yourself?" In the midst of gaining information for yourself, try to move toward understanding, thereby communicating love and support to your son or daughter. As you listen with all seriousness, you may also be helping your child to clarify his or her own experiences. Regardless of other feelings that you may be having, you are in fact helping to bring yourself closer to your son or daughter.

Talk about why you are discussing this right now. "What were your reasons for initiating this with me?" Or: "You were really mad at me when you said that. I wish it could have come out in some other way, but here it is. In addition to being mad at me, is there something else you want from me in telling me about it?" Or: "I'm sorry I had to get information like this from someone else. Tell me what's been going on with you and what has stood in the way of your speaking to me about it."

In the midst of this discussion, be honest with your son or daughter. You are having thoughts and feelings yourself, and it is important for you to express them. "This is very difficult for me. It really hurts." "I find myself feeling guilty and blaming myself but feeling mad at you at the same time." "I'm trying, but I find it very difficult to understand." Being a person with feelings, expressing them will be more helpful in the relationship than trying to pretend that you don't have them. However, it may certainly be possible that the strength of your feelings and your confusion may lead you to say things that you later (a few minutes, hours, days) wish you hadn't said. You may feel bad about it, and the words may have been angering or hurting to your child, but words can always be taken back. In this we are all in the same human boat. It is then important to say what this is like for you to your son or daughter. "When I said . . . , I was really furious at you (or "feeling panicky," or "devastated," or whatever), and I am really sorry that I said it (or "said it the way I did"). It expressed my real *feelings* at the time, but it is not the main way that I view you and feel about you. Would you try to understand and forgive me for it?"

Keep in mind during the early conversation or conversations the differences in the possible meanings of words, feelings, and behaviors of children of different ages and circumstances, as we discussed earlier. Keeping these in mind, try to discover what your child is actually trying to communicate to you and what the child wants from you at this time. "When you use the word 'gay' (or 'homosexual') about yourself, what specifically do you mean?" "When you say that you and . . . did this together, how long has it been going on? Is it something you have done just once or twice or has it been a lot? Does that mean that you are really sexually attracted to that person and only to persons of the same sex, or have you also had feelings toward the opposite sex?" Or for an older child, "Are you in love, and/or are you living with someone now?" To repeat the earlier point in this chapter, your son or daughter may be talking with you about some homosexual feelings or some homosexual behavior and about confusion concerning himself or herself, but he or she may not in fact be homosexual. Or he or she may be. It is very important to begin to make these distinctions.

Again, we realize that we are proposing something that is extremely difficult for parents and often for the child, too. You may not want to ask. You may be afraid to hear the answer. Your son or daughter may not really want to respond to you. But the subject is up and out, and the reality of it needs to be clarified and a certain minimum amount of information is necessary. Of course, questions asking for too much minute detail should be avoided. The young person or adult still has a right to privacy about some intimate matters just as you yourself do.

The conversation then leads to open discussion about what your son or daughter wants or expects of you. This knowledge can help you shape your further responses and once again assist in the relationship at a particularly difficult time.

Especially at the younger ages, early and middle teens and occasionally in the older teens and early twenties, a son or daughter may mainly desire an increased understanding. "What do these feelings, this behavior, mean about *me?* I'm confused about *myself.* Why am I like this? What is my future going to be? I feel so bad about myself." The young persons may or may not want to change their feelings and behavior, but the fundamental project is self-understanding. Realizing that they have their parents' genuine support at this time is extremely important for them. If they gain significant self-understanding, it may not make them "change into heterosexuals," but some of them may discover that they are not truly homosexual in the first place. At any rate, self-understanding, insight, a good self-concept are essential for any human being. This is the beginning point. Most teenagers will need their parents' guidance. Where do they get this kind of assistance? Some of it may come from parents themselves through just such discussions as we are trying to describe here, but much help can come from talking with a minister or other professional counselor. "Aye, there's the rub." As a matter of fact, there are a couple of rubs.

The first is how the parents make the suggestion. If it is in panic and anger, with bribes or threats, the young person may rebel and not really go for the help that is needed and that at one level of the person's being is genuinely wanted. A better response of the parents is: "It sounds as if you are very confused about the whole matter yourself and feel bad about yourself, and that you are really asking for some way to understand yourself better. Also, although we want to continue to talk with you ourselves, there are probably some things you might not feel free to say to us and probably could to someone else. What do you think about our trying to find someone you could talk to?"

The second rub is whom to talk to. Your minister or some other minister? Maybe. For young people to whom the Christian faith is meaningful, who had or still have some relationship with the church, there can be some advantages in talking with a minister. But how the minister views homosexuality, and especially homosexuals, and to some extent whether the minister has training in counseling can be factors that need to be taken into consideration. Some ministers have feelings of revulsion and condemnation and this will rule them out automatically. And frankly, some ministers' own personal *feelings* become more important to them than their theological position. Can the minister understand people who are different from himself or herself, be noncondemnatory, work helpfully with them, not be overly anxious, be compassionate, not be authoritarian? These are the especially critical factors.

Interestingly, more than one gay person has reported to us that most ministers with whom they have had anything to do have not been openly condemning, but rather have tended to pass off too easily what the young person is telling them. "I've known your family and I've known you for so many years, and you all are good solid people. A number of people have these feelings. It's just a phase. You'll get over it." While these statements may in fact be descriptive of some young persons, it is clearly not descriptive of others and can be hurtfully misleading. It is not taking the young person seriously to respond too quickly in this way even when it might be the case. One or more of three possibilities seem to lead to this type of response. First, the minister has little awareness of what homosexuality really is. Second, the response is a part of the minister's own denial and inability and unwillingness to deal seriously with this person about this issue. Third, the reasoning may go like this: "Homosexuality is depravity. I know you and you are not depraved. Therefore, it's impossible for you to be homosexual." Beginning with a false assumption, these ministers reach a conclusion with tragic implications for the person wanting help.

Nevertheless, numerous young people and adults who have been confused or disturbed by their homosexual feelings and behavior, who have been in the process of trying to clarify their sexual identity, or who have been afraid to tell their parents or who have told and are now in a situation of distress with their parents, have talked with their minister or another minister and have experienced compassion and personal support and have gained clarity for themselves. Even ministers who genuinely understand the Bible to be condemning homosexuality and/or homosexual acts, and who themselves do see this as sinful, may be compassionate human beings, good listeners, accurate in their feedback, and able to facilitate the person's self-exploration and decision-making. Parents, too, have received help.

What about a psychiatrist or a psychologist or other well-trained professional counselor? They also vary. Don't depend on the yellow pages. Find out. Avoid two extremes: the ones who start from the premise that all homosexuals should be changed into heterosexuals and the ones who too easily and quickly say: "You are okay just like you are. You just need to feel better about yourself." Rather, search for the competent professional who is also a compassionate human being. It is important that you select one who always begins by helping the person to explore feelings, background, relationships, conflicts, needs, the meaning of behavior. Then on the basis of such work, this counselor helps the person set goals and assists in the achievement of them, the person being guided, of course, by the therapist's own human and professional experience.

Some young people, especially those who are in their twenties or older, realize that ultimately the parents may find out about their sexual orientation one way or another. Therefore, they believe that it is only right for the parents to hear it directly. Even in those instances where there is tension, uneasiness, or even some amount of anger and alienation, the young people want a better relationship with their parents. When they talk with their parents about being gay, it is primarily a matter of sharing a significant area of their lives, of reducing the tension of living a lie with them (although obviously other tensions are created), and, it is hoped, of being accepted as a member of the family as they are. This doesn't mean that because they are older they have no confusion or problems or low self-esteem, but it is to say that by this time some of them have had one or more real love attachments and they may actually be living with someone at the time. The gay life is already well established and they have no intent to change.

There are several things for parents to avoid if possible. One is the use of threats, bribery, pleading, trying to evoke their son's or daughter's guilt as a means of getting the person to change, to stop doing this. As we have emphasized, there will probably be shock, confusion, a sense of panic, anger, some complex reaction out of which they are likely to say all sorts of things. It is all right to express those feelings, but parents can also do so in ways that allow them to move into the more constructive conversations that we have been trying to describe. There can be no continued meaningful conversations if a father bans a son or daughter from the home with word not to return until he or she has changed. Seeing a minister or a psychiatrist under threat will not bring about what the parents desire. Many young people have felt even more alienated and angry as a result of their parents' not too subtle bribes and bargaining. This is not to eliminate earnest conversation on the part of the parents in terms of what they would like to see the child do when these parents' desires are expressed in clear and straightforward terms and are understood simply for what they are, the parents' desires and best advice.

It is also important to avoid the suggestion that is still all too often offered to a son: "You just need to date more. If you could only find a good woman, it would be different. If you only had a woman to make love to, you wouldn't have these feelings any longer." And the same to the daughter. Too much pain and damage has occurred this way. Many young people genuinely want to please their parents. They may therefore try the suggested courses of action, all too frequently to their own and someone else's detriment. Especially hurtful have been those situations when, in confusion and under parental pressure, a homosexual person marries, only to have it all fall apart later. Some young persons whose sexual pattern is not set, while in therapy with a competent professional, may in fact begin to move in these directions, learning to be more comfortable with occasions of intimacy and sharing with the opposite sex, beginning to feel some affection, growing increasingly able to express it physically, and so forth. But as general advice, this can lead to great stress, anxiety, pain, and sometimes a shattered life, increased feelings of failure, and even suicidal feelings.

For any parent who has just discovered that a child is homosexual, the first order of business is to be a certain quality of person. This is the person who can still love and communicate even in the midst of a shocking and painful experience. The crucial question is, Can you be who you are and still be the parents of children who are as they *are*, even when they are quite different from you?

4. Where Does the Fault Belong?

If indeed your child is homosexual, when the initial shock of disclosure or discovery has somewhat abated and the period of denial is over, it is quite usual to begin to have some very angry feelings. Sometimes these feelings come out in a blast at the child who has revealed a hidden self to you. Sometimes the anger is not available for expression and the feeling which you are aware of is pain that is experienced physically as well as emotionally. There can also be a depressed feeling that comes from held-in anger. It takes so much energy to contain it that the result is fatigue and often feelings of tension as well.

"After Jan told me she was gay, I was numb for days. Then I began to clean my house like I had never cleaned house before. I was out in the backyard one morning hanging up some curtains I had washed. I was jabbing the clothespins on real hard. When I came into the house my husband said I should look in the mirror, that I looked furious. I did and he was right. I began to cry, really hard sobs, and beat the kitchen table with my fists. It really was good to get that out. It surprised me that I felt stronger."

Initially, it is often felt that it is not safe or appropriate to allow the angry feelings to be openly directed toward the son or daughter who has apparently chosen to be different. So there is a tendency to displace much of that negative feeling onto "evil" influences around that person and outside the home. Even in the midst of a great deal of hurt and anger and disappointment there is a very natural tendency on the part of parents to rush to the defense of their children. The younger the child, the more often this is the case.

Knowledge of a son's or daughter's chosen sex preference is often experienced as a loss of the total person. Therefore the anger accompanying that experience is as though "they" took your son or daughter from you. In the case of older, more mature young people and adults the opinion of the parents is more apt to be that the person simply did not resist temptation and therefore took himself or herself away from the parents. The thinking here often still tends to be focused on the influences of persons outside the family, however. The content of parents' thoughts can be very vengeful. This is all a part of our very common human reluctance to let go of those whom we love—either in death or in a direction we don't want them to go. You are not "bad" human beings to have such angry, hate-filled thoughts. To think and feel is not to act and this is an important distinction to make at this time. It is simply a part of the process and this, too, passes with time and continuing to work through the feelings and confusion.

We human beings have a great need to have reasons and explanations, to find meanings for events. Your speculations about how it all happened in the case of your homosexual son or daughter may have many elements of blaming. Blaming is a part of the search for meaning and we thrust onto another the responsibility for an event that we experience as hurtful. When we are hurt and angry we want to accuse and blame, and frequently there are strong feelings of wanting to punish the sources which we have decided at this point may be the cause of our pain and loss. To discover a cause other than oneself does give a temporary sense of relief.

"There *has* to be a reason why this absolutely normal little boy has grown up to be gay. He had a happy, uneventful childhood. He did not have any trauma in his young life that hundreds of kids haven't had, too. We were reasonably good parents. All I can think of is that he went to a big university far away from home. He was young and vulnerable and lonely. He was taken advantage of. That university had a responsibility to provide a decent place for shy kids to meet and get to know each other. They are thrown on their own at such a tender age. We trusted that school and it was a terrible mistake. Too much sexual propaganda is allowed."

The intensity of feeling that accompanies blaming can be dismaying, even frightening. Parents speak of wanting to attack verbally, and sometimes physically, those whom they believe influenced or caused their son or daughter to become what they didn't want a child of theirs to be. There are imaginings and fantasies of harsh accusations and punishments of those held responsible.

"It's the rotten newspapers and TV. They glorify sin and immorality. Can't turn on the set without some 'expert' talking about how many people are acting in what I consider sinful ways and therefore it's okay for everybody. The media should have some sense of responsibility for upgrading the moral fiber of this country. What chance do parents have to raise kids decently with all that corruption? Sometimes, and especially right now, I'd like to get my hands on the guys who allow that stuff on the air. They'd have another think coming!"

Another group that is blamed not so much for *influencing* the young as for *not* influencing them at all is the church, particularly that segment of the church labeled "liberal." The criticism often is leveled at the so-called permissiveness perceived in some theological teachings. A mother says: "It is clear to me that we have been betrayed by our own church. They have actually allowed groups of homosexuals to use our church building for meetings. I was against it when the deacons voted to give permission. I'm not sure I can support my church ever again because now it is a personal thing. If my son had had the clear-cut guidance of the church during his formative years, this might not have happened. Instead, doubt was planted in his mind and they encouraged a questioning of the high standards which the church ought to uphold."

For many parents there is anger and bewilderment at what appears to them to be a failure of school and church to support and reinforce the principles to which they, the parents, adhere. There are many expressions of helplessness and rage as these parents explore memories of their children and young people in church and school.

For some parents there is a profound sense of desertion by God accompanied in some instances with intense anger. "All my life I have been faithful to God and my church. I have loved my family as best I knew how and saw to it that we were a praying, church-attending family. And it wasn't just show either. My daughter was a leader in the youth group from junior high on and we all supported her. I feel God has let me down, and the ones I love. Where was God's protection for my girl? My faith is utterly destroyed; I can no longer pray; there is nothing to pray to." This particular mother went through a deep depression with many expressions of anger at what she perceived as God's letting her down by not directing her daughter in the ways she believed her daughter would find happiness. With a patient and kind husband and a skilled minister she came to an acceptance of God's presence which allowed her to be comforted again in her now stronger faith. She grieves still for her daughter, but the relationship is open and growing.

A father casting about for the reason that his son was homosexual remembered his dislike for his son's circle of friends in grade school.

"If it hadn't been for that bunch of sissies he ran around with, none of this would have happened. I never did like any of them. They were always talking, making noise, not out playing ball every day like normal kids. Their mothers should have cut out all that artsy-craftsy stuff. My boy probably wouldn't have been in all those plays in high school if he hadn't been influenced by that gang. He could have played team sports and learned how to be a real man. That bunch of kids and their mothers ruined my son."

Organized groups of homosexuals, unorganized gay persons, people both lay and professional who have anything positive to say about homosexuals, come in for a scathing attack by some parents. For some it appears that these groups and/or individuals encourage and promote homosexuality. In actuality, of course, the groups and individuals respond to the needs of persons already homosexual. To parents who are earnestly searching for reasons that their son or daughter is homosexual the distinction is not readily clear. There is certainly enough misinformation published and talked about that otherwise thoughtful parents cannot be faulted for feeling for a period of time that their son or daughter may have been victimized and unwittingly coerced into a life he or she would not have chosen if left alone.

Ideally, a dialogue continues between the homosexual person and the parents. As the course of this particular grief is run, there can be opportunities to explore and evaluate the groups or persons whom parents blame. Perhaps some of them can be eliminated as inappropriate targets. As these targets are eliminated new ones may occur. Interspersed with this blame-placing outside the home will be blame-placing very close to home, including one's spouse and self. This will be discussed in Chapter 5.

The process of working through the various stages of this grief will include times of relief, even calm, and then going back through some of the thoughts and feelings anew. It is hoped that the going back is not a return to exactly the same point, but the necessary reworking of some of the same issues and feelings from a different vantage point, with some new insights. These insights are best gained by earnest, open talking with the son or daughter, one's husband or wife, and perhaps other family members, friends, minister, or another professional care giver.

5. Where Did We Go Wrong?

One of the most agonizing questions parents ask themselves when a child reveals his or her homosexuality to them is, "What did I do wrong?" or "What did we do wrong?" It is a time of searching out reasons why this event happened to this child, to this family. Was it the year he was in the nursery school when his mother worked full time? Should Father have taken more time from work for fishing and ball playing? Should Mother have insisted on keeping her in dresses?

And don't forget "odd" Uncle Hubert. Maybe there is an inherited weakness somewhere. On whose side of the family?

There is an inevitable human tendency to oscillate between blame and guilt in this process: one day "knowing" it was the way the other parent behaved toward the child and the next day "knowing" that it was neglect and carelessness on one's own part.

It is not at all unusual to remember some guilt-ridden behavior of the past and decide that punishment is being visited through this terrible happening.

A father confessed for the first time his heavy burden of guilt for an affair which he was involved in years ago while he was a traveling salesman. He remembered staying away from home longer than he needed to in order to spend time with his girl friend. His preoccupation with her increasing demands for more time and finally her insistence that he leave his wife had left him with little energy or interest in his family for a period of about a year. He remembered vividly a scene where he had slapped his small son for demanding that he come outside and look at fireflies. He recalled with tears in his eyes the tears in the eyes of his child. Could all of this be the reason? Was this son's homosexuality his own punishment for being an unfaithful husband and neglectful father? There are certainly many bargains made around "I will never again . . . if only he will change and not be homosexual anymore," or "I promise I will . . . if only."

A detailed review of the child's development since birth is frequently undertaken by one parent or both parents. Often enough some lacks are recognized as real and there is the sorrow that comes with such a realization. It is well to remember at this time a universal truth: no parent is perfect. Mistakes made when parents are young and uninformed are often made in the context of loving care, are forgivable, and far more often than not have not been detrimental.

Ruminations in the night are common. Lying awake hour after hour and going over the child's whole life or perhaps focusing on a few painful events often occurs. Another variation is going to sleep fairly easily and then awakening in the wee small hours of the morning to remember and agonize. It is during these dark and lonely times that bitterness brews and corrodes. Anger with child, spouse, and self churns and stirs the blaming and faultfinding. The term "dark night of the soul" is certainly applicable to this stage of the process. For some there will be many repetitions of such nights and for others they will be few or sporadic. Each parent will have his or her own timetable of this process and the timetables will likely not coincide. It is a time to be tolerant of each other's differences and feelings and the varying intensities as well. No two persons go through any emotional experience in the same way or for the same length of time.

It is certainly helpful if parents at this stage can talk to each other freely and openly. In other circumstances, such as illness or bereavement, there is the same need, but the opportunity to talk feelings out with many persons is usually possible. Family and friends gather around and are readily available. But parents who have found out that their son or daughter is homosexual often feel isolated, as we have said earlier. However, for many parents clergy are a present help in time of need. In many cities there are groups made up of the parents of homosexual men and women. These groups can be very helpful as a forum to discuss feelings. But most parents of homosexuals have only each other, or think they do, and that fact puts tremendous and sometimes overwhelming pressure on the relationship. The anger can get very personal and the blaming can be vitriolic. Other issues typically are brought in when the conflict escalates.

"You criticized every boy she ever dated. None of them was good enough for your daughter. And you told her a lot of frightening things about men. How do you think that made me feel? As a matter of fact you always put me down, and not just in front of her but in front of everyone. I've resented your treatment of me for years."

The blamed one can counterattack or withdraw in wounded silence, or courageously examine the statement and allow for the possibility of a need for correction in the parental relationship. No figures are available for the number of marriages that fail following (not as a result of) the revelation of homosexuality, but it does occur just as it does following the death of a child. The opportunity which this crisis presents (and all crises *do* present opportunities) is to look anew at the marital and family relationships and do some perhaps long overdue evaluating. Where there is openness to change, there is life and possibility for the future. Talking it out is the way to change.

If there is only one parent in the family or if only one parent is informed and the information is being kept from the other parent for one reason or another, it is a greatly increased burden.

Perhaps other children in the family are aware of the sexual preference of their sibling and can interact with each other and with one or both parents in a way that can be mutually helpful. As we mentioned in Chapter 1, a brother or sister is often the first to know.

The issues of what went wrong are best struggled with verbally and with someone who can really listen. If a spouse *will* not talk, it is desirable to seek out a good and trusted confidant: friend, another family member, a minister. Disturbing thoughts get less disturbing when shared. If the judgment is made that there is no one close to turn to, a professional care giver should be considered. Sessions during which thoughts and feelings can be expressed concerning possible errors in child-rearing and exploring family relationships could relieve some pressure. Feelings about spouse and self can be explored. One cannot expect that as a result of the counseling blame will be pinpointed or any past errors corrected. Yet the process of going over the many thoughts and emotions out loud in the presence of an understanding other person is the beginning of working through the difficult phase of looking for what went wrong.

Do not overlook the real possibility of help to be found in talking to your homosexual son or daughter. Most revelations of homosexuality are made by young people or adults who want to live honestly with themselves and their families. They have frequently gone through a process of working through a lot of emotional turmoil themselves before you were told. It is likely that you can profitably share your misgivings with your child and get helpful feedback.

Bill reported on a conversation with his mother who had been widowed when Bill was seven and who had raised him alone on a small salary. "I've thought and thought about all this, Bill, and I just feel sure that if only I had let you play football when you were in high school, you wouldn't be like this. I remember well telling you on your first day at the high school that football scared me to death and I said you just could not play. You didn't say a word and I remember feeling uneasy, but glad that you hadn't argued. I wish I could do it all over again; I would certainly let you play any sport you wanted to." Bill smiled at his mother, and putting his hands on her shoulders, he replied: "Mom, I remember that day too. I was so relieved to be *ordered* not to play football. I never wanted to. I was little, remember? And I wasn't very coordinated either. I was afraid they would make hamburger out of me if I ever got out on that field. You only beat me to the punch. I wanted to play in the band more than anything and I couldn't have done both."

In further discussion with her son this mother was able finally to rest in the knowledge that she hadn't been a perfect parent, but was seen by her son as having done the best she could, which, at times, was just right.

Self-blame and guilt are natural and quite common. With the self-searching, and especially, as we have already suggested in regard to other feelings, searching aloud with your spouse, other family members, friends, a minister, a professional counselor, your unrealistic self-blame and guilt will gradually diminish to the vanishing point, and behavior that has stimulated appropriate guilt can be forgiven by a spouse, the child, God, and, importantly, yourself.

6. If He or She "Only Loved Us . . ."

Many parents at one time or another feel angry with their homosexual sons and daughters for their *being* homosexual or sometimes for *telling* them, the parents, about the fact. Some parents appear not to experience such anger, but most do. In Chapter 2 we reported the first direct verbal response of one father to his son after he found out: "It's a good thing you're not around here. I'd kill you." Another young man tells of his father's outbursts of rage in which the father calls his son all sorts of names. Some young people have been angrily banished from their homes. "You can come back when you've changed to how you're supposed to be!"

Anger is a natural human emotion when we are deeply hurt or frustrated or afraid. Anger toward someone else may also sometimes be that which is felt toward oneself but is shifted to another target. Youth or young adults who are homosexual and who are telling or writing their parents about their sexual orientation often say, "Now please don't be mad, but . . ." Of course, what they are expressing is their own discomfort with their parents' angry displeasure, but naturally they are making a request that is unreasonable for a large majority of parents. They *are* hurt, or frustrated, or afraid, or some combination of these, and therefore they probably also are going to be angry. Although most of us parents have properly understood our task, as we discussed earlier, as assisting our children to move from independence to autonomy, giving them more and more freedom as they are ready for it, there are numerous times when they exercise their freedom in ways that don't meet our image, built up over the years, of who *our* child is going to be and how he or she is going to act. We are angry over our loss of control, even though in our better moments we have always known that we could not control them forever. We have just always dreamed that they would exercise control over their own lives in the ways that we would control them if we could. Oh, parenting! The joys and sorrows, the satisfactions and the pain, our own very real conflicts. This is just the way most of us are, so often experiencing our children's variance from us as if it were something done personally *against* us.

Now a son or daughter has told you that he or she is gay. Gay? Most parents don't even like the word. Often enough one of the first reactions is, "Why is our child doing this to us?" It is not unusual that when parents are hit so hard by their shattered dreams, the sense of the loss of their son or daughter, the feeling of helplessness in a situation where control has slipped away from them, they shoot at targets wherever they can find them. It is someone else's fault, and they are angry with "them" (Chapter 4). It is their own fault as parents (Chapter 5). It is the kids' fault. "They've always known what we've stood for. They've been raised in the church. They're bound to have assimilated the values we've held to be most important. Therefore, they know that this is wrong. They must be doing this to hurt us. If they only loved us, they wouldn't be this way."

For so many parents it comes as such a brutal shock. Your sons or daughters may have been so "good" in so many ways. They have been obedient. They have seemed to care about what you think.

They have gone to church. You have certainly been led to believe that their value system, their ideals, their faith in God was the same, or at least similar, to yours.

But homosexuality is such a *radical* difference. It feels like a stab in the back. "Have we been wrong about them all this time? How long has this hidden rebellion been going on? Can we trust them now when they say they truly love us and don't want to hurt us? We're not sure. Not now, anyway. We *do* hurt. They must have known how this would make us feel. If they *really* loved us, they wouldn't have *done* this to us."

Anger is understandable. It is a frequent reaction to frustration and hurt and fear. But along with the anger are often the thinking components of the reaction as we have been describing it. This type of thinking has two flaws in it. First, it assumes intentionality on the son's or daughter's part in *being* homosexual, and second, it assumes a single cause-effect system in human behavior. "If you really loved us, you wouldn't have *chosen* to feel, act, *be* this way. Your lack of love for us, your rebellion against us, has produced this behavior, and in turn is proof that you don't love us." None of the elements of this circular argument holds up under the facts. As we shall try to explain in detail in Chapter 8, the human condition of being homosexual is not a condition that is chosen. Whatever is involved in any one person's being homosexual, the influences started very early in that person's life and developed over many years, covering the years of childhood dependence and then moving on into adolescence. Certain *acts*, indeed, are chosen, but the *condition* is *not* in any simple and self-conscious way. In addition, human behavior is so complex that it rarely if ever is accurate to suggest a simple cause-effect product. It makes no more sense to say, "If they really loved us, they wouldn't be this way, or they would change," than it does to say, "If I'd only played ball more with my son, or, "if I hadn't let her run around and play with those little boys all the time, she wouldn't be this way." These explanations of the human condition and human behavior are too simple.

Anger is understandable. This sort of *thinking*, however, doesn't fit the facts. Now let's be thoroughly honest. There *may* be angry or rebellious elements in a son's or daughter's homosexual behavior, some of the ways in which it is done, or the setting or manner in which the child tells the parents about it. Many children of all ages, heterosexual and homosexual, do get angry with their parents, and their sexual acting out may be one form of the expression of their feelings toward them. This is another issue. It is not *the* reason they *are* homosexual. The anger of your homosexual son or daughter toward you and now your anger toward your son or daughter needs to be traced to its roots and dealt with openly on that basis if you are to have a good relationship with one another. However, it is unrealistic for you to expect that when your child's anger diminishes and the rebellion vanishes the child will therefore automatically become heterosexual *because he or she now loves you.* (Even in the anger and rebellion, by the way, your son or daughter probably never *did* stop loving you.)

There is another difficulty in these early days following the discovery of a child's homosexuality. The "if he only loved us, he wouldn't be this way" as an expression of hurt and anger may all too easily slide over into the attempt to create guilt in the child in order to manipulate him. Having had the experience of losing control over their child, some parents now try to regain it in this way.

A man in his late twenties was referred to one of the authors of this book by a minister, who reported that according to the parents their son had been having some trouble with homosexual feelings and wanted help with this problem. Would we see him? Yes. He came in. As is the usual procedure in such a referral by someone else, we began something like this. "You know that Reverend Johnson called and told us what your parents had told him. That puts us about three steps away from *you,* and yet *you're* the one who's here. We wonder if you'd be willing to tell us as honestly as you can your own real reasons for coming to see us."

The young man seemed to be surprised by this approach, because he first looked somewhat startled, then he hung his head, looked a bit sheepish, then looked back up and said, "Because my mother wanted me to." Our next question had to be, "But what is it *you* want?" As it turned out, he had not been "bothered" recently by homosexual feelings. He had had them for about fifteen years and had finally come to the conclusion that he really was gay and that this was the way he wanted to be. He was in love with a man with whom he had been living for several months. He was well established in the homosexual community. He didn't desire to change his sexual orientation at all. But he also genuinely loved his parents. Their approach had been that if he *really* cared for them and the whole family, he would get help to try to change. But he didn't *want* to change. A terrible conflict for him! He wanted to be as he *was,* but he also wanted to "prove" his love for his parents and his desire to please them. The danger was that if he didn't try to change, they would *never* be pleased with him. The alternative, which the young man expressed, was his desire that they love him as their son as he was and that he be allowed to be as much a part of the family as he had been when they didn't know about his being homosexual.

Most parents feel angry in the early days (weeks, sometimes months) after discovering that their son or daughter is homosexual. This is understandable, and their children need to appreciate the fact that given who their parents are, their anger is natural. But how are parents to express their anger?

If over the long haul you truly want to have a good relationship with your son or daughter, try to avoid three responses. First, violence, name-calling, personal abuse, threats, banishment are *all* counterproductive. They express the anger, but they don't change your son's or daughter's homosexuality. They don't motivate him or her to change. They may often drive a wedge more deeply into the relationship between you.

Second, pretending that you are *not* angry doesn't work, because the anger continues to fester inside you, causing you more pain, and it inevitably comes out in disguised forms (against each other as parents, hurting behavior toward the child, depression). One mother in her rage wrote frequent vitriolic, accusatory, demeaning letters to her son. He finally responded by telling her that they weren't going to get anywhere as long as she expressed herself that way to him. Then on her birthday he sent her a present. The very next letter thanked him for remembering her, and the whole tone of this and the following letters was sweet, filled with news, just like the "old" times, as if nothing had happened. But something *had* happened, and it stretches the imagination too far to think that her feelings had changed so suddenly and radically. She had gotten the point that what she had been doing was destructive to the relationship, and she apparently really didn't want that. So she changed her behavior. But we believe that there must still be some anger there. She and her son both need to realize that if there is, it needs to be out in the open between them, although in a different form from before.

Third, given the opportunity to think through what we have been discussing in this chapter, we see that to express anger through the "if you only loved us" statement and our attempt to react to our helplessness in this new situation by that kind of language may be guilt-producing and just plain doesn't work.

If you are angry, just say so to your son or daughter. Try to be in touch with the intensity of the hurt, the shattered dreams, the frustration, the wanting it to be different but feeling helpless and afraid. These feelings should be shared between husband and wife and between parent and child. Remember, these are the original source of your anger, and when these other emotions and the experiences that produce them are fully felt and talked about and begin to diminish, the anger also will gradually diminish and usually disappear. Also be aware of the fact that a part of love is revealing ourselves even when we are afraid of the consequences, even when it will make us vulnerable, even when we are aware that there will be hurt involved. Sons and daughters are usually aware of this when they tell their parent about their homosexual orientation. When parents then also make themselves vulnerable to their sons and daughters as they speak of their hurt and fear and disappointment, the anger toward one another in this situation loses its power.

7. What Will People Think?

"Hello, Ed. It's good to see you. How're your kids?"

"Just fine, Joe. How's your family?"

"Great. Joe, Jr., got married a few weeks ago, you know. We went up to Seattle for the wedding. It was a great time. Joe really got himself a fine girl. By the way, has old Bill gotten married yet?"

"No, not yet."

"Well, he had better hurry up. He's twenty-eight or twenty-nine now, isn't he?"

"Twenty-nine."

"Well, he's a nice-looking kid, and he's a fine person, too. You're lucky to have a son like that. Some girl will get him before long."

"Yeah."

"I've gotta be moving on. Good to see you, Ed. Tell your wife and kids hello for me."

"Yeah, nice to see you, too, Joe. Same to your family."

The men move away from each other on the street.

How it hurts! I don't want to see anyone I know. I can't look them in the eye. I feel so ashamed. They're bound to be able to read it in my face. So, little Joe got married. I remember getting the invitation now. I felt real pleased then. Thought there was still hope for Bill. That was just about a month before he told us. *My* son! In love with another man! Been living with him for a year. We knew he had a roommate. But they're lovers! Why do people have to ask about him? Why do they want to know if he's married yet? I lie through my teeth! There's no *way* I can tell them the truth! What would they think about us? About Bill? How could I call on customers and expect to get any kind of reception? We'd never be able to hold our heads up in public anymore. We've practically stopped going to church the last few weeks. I feel so out of place there now. If they only knew! They couldn't understand. I already feel as if everybody's eyes are glued on me when I walk in anyway. I just can't take it. Somehow it all feels so dirty. It's like *I'd* done something.

"Has old Bill gotten married yet? He'd better hurry up." A parent *feels* the unspoken message: "There's something wrong with him. There's something wrong with you." There's a feeling of shame that somehow you've betrayed your family, your church, the human race. You just can't shake it.

Somehow this feels different from guilt. Guilt is our awareness that we have done something wrong that we have actually been responsible for. We have violated a standard, broken a rule or law. Whether anyone else knows it or not, we know it within ourselves. Shame is the feeling that we have in the face of our failure to live up to an ideal, and somehow it has something to do with the way other people would think and feel about us if they knew about it. Guilt is internalized; *I* see it as wrong regardless of what other people think. Shame is what I feel when other people recognize or see that I don't live up to the community ideal.

In the instance of your son's or daughter's being homosexual, Ed's feelings are somewhat realistic. He and his wife and other members of his family have the same unspoken yet unquestioned expectations of the greatest percentage of society: children will grow up heterosexual, will probably marry (and are deviant and somewhat suspect if they don't), and will probably have children. This pattern is a social ideal that most of us have unconsciously adopted as our own, as unfair as it actually is to a lot of people when we stop to think about it. Nevertheless, the failure to *be* this ideal is a part of the homosexual person's own grappling with identity and the feeling of shame, feeling very bad about one's self, having the very low self-esteem that is such a characteristic part of the reactions of these persons to the growing awareness of their sexual orientation, at least during the early stages and for some for a much longer period of time. Being linked together as we are in families, and often enough tending to look at families as a single entity within which differences are not expected, other persons within the family feel shame also. Therefore, homosexuality, like a variety of other "family failures" (alcoholism and mental illness, for example), is to be kept a secret. Other people must never know, or we'll all be social outcasts. What will people think about us? We predict that they will think about us as we are now thinking and feeling about ourselves—shame, that we are bad parents, that something mysterious and wrong has been going on in our house.

A young man reported his observations of his parents' reactions. The father particularly had almost a sense of desperation about the possibility that someone in the town would find out. He repeatedly told his wife: "Don't dare tell *anyone*. If *anyone* finds out about this, I'm going to have to leave. I just can't face people if they know this." Here is being expressed the depth of the shame, the intensity of his own terrible feelings, the social fear. But he is also stating it in such a way that it comes across as a threat to his wife. "If you tell, I'll have to leave you." And so this threat becomes a barrier between them at a time when they need each other more than ever. The mother wanted to try to work it all through with her son as quickly as possible so she could truly accept him in an easy relationship once again. But the father was saying, "The more you try to understand, the worse you make it for me." The mother was being pushed into a position of great conflict: even in her hurt and disappointment she had the urge to understand and accept her own son, but she was being told that to do so would be to push her husband away from her. What a tragically difficult situation!

It is not unusual for parents to agree with each other that they will tell no one else. So at a time when they desperately need the loving, if not totally understanding, support of other family members, of friends and neighbors and fellow workers, of the church, they keep it a secret. The end result is an intensification of the feelings of isolation that they already have. The parents just referred to above said: "There's literally *no one* we can talk to about this. We don't know a single family in this town who's experienced this. There's no one."

People feel as if they must keep shame to themselves, and yet the sense of isolation which is intensified by keeping the secret further feeds the intensification of the feeling of shame. It is a destructive trap. Isolation also leads to a breakdown of reality-testing, that normal sharing of things we have heard, of our perceptions and interpretations of all sorts of things, as a part of everyday conversation. As we express these, some of them are confirmed, but we also hear conflicting information and differing perceptions and interpretations. This constant testing and retesting of our sense of things is necessary to keep our thinking clear and reasonably accurate, and thus to reduce feelings of suspicion, fear, threat, and inappropriate anger that otherwise would have free rein and make our lives unhappy and ineffective.

We have already indicated the importance of parents' talking with each other, with other members of the family, with selected good and trusted friends, perhaps with their minister or a professional counselor. How blessed also are those parents who have within their local church congregation a prayer group, a Sunday school class, or a small sharing group where they can tell the others that their child is homosexual. They can express to these concerned persons what they themselves are experiencing, and receive from this group love and understanding and continued support.

When the parents of the young man we have been talking about told him they didn't know any family who had had this experience, he immediately told them of several within their circle of friends and acquaintances. They were not as alone as they thought.

When some parents begin with dread to tell their other children that their brother or sister is homosexual, at least fairly often these other children will respond, "Oh, I've thought (or "known") that for a long time."

Of course, you have to face social reality. Some people *won't* understand. Some people *may* pull away from you. Some minister *may* be condemnatory. Some customer may *not* buy from you anymore. None of us has control over the thoughts, feelings, and behavior of other people. They will say what they'll say, just as they do in a number of other situations. To this extent, there is some risk for you. But there is much more risk in allowing your feelings of wanting to keep it all hidden to dictate your behavior to the point that you hide and lie and pretend. This type of behavior is usually very damaging to persons and relationships.

Therefore, to whom shall we tell what? With some exceptions, it is important that both parents and every member of the immediate family and other members of the family whom you would expect to be seeing be informed. As we indicated in Chapter 1, it is fairly common for a homosexual young person or young adult to tell a brother or sister first, and then tell a parent or the parents. It is also more frequent, according to our experience, for the child to tell the mother first rather than the father or the two of them together, or merely to tell the mother but not the father. This observation of ours is at least in line with, although not proved by, Bell and Weinberg's study of the homosexual persons themselves (Alan P. Bell and Martin S. Weinberg, *Homosexualities;* Simon & Schuster, 1978). Forty percent of the white males reported that they thought their mothers definitely knew about their sexual orientation, while only 33 percent thought their fathers knew (pp. 63–64). Almost 50 percent of the white females thought their mothers definitely knew and 40 percent thought their fathers knew (pp. 66–67). This is not the same as their having specifically *told* their mothers and/or fathers, and, of course, some of them may *not* have told and are guessing wrong about their parents' knowledge. But it is interesting that with both male and female, it is the mothers who are pointed to more often as knowing, and it is the mothers in our experience who time and again are pointed to by their children as probably being more understanding and willing to work through their feelings and the issues openly.

However, *both* parents need to know. If a mother says, "We mustn't tell your father; I don't know what he'd do," or a father says, "We can't tell your mother; it'll just kill her," you need to take a hard look at what that may mean. First, this type of response on the part of a parent may reflect that something is already quite wrong with the relationship between the husband and wife. Second, it may create (or strengthen) a divisive coalition in the family, pitting one parent and the child against the other parent. This speaks to the inadequacy of the ways in which husband and wife meet, or fail to meet, each other's needs. Finally, trying to keep the secret from one parent causes additional stress within the family, as does any pattern of covering up and withholding. A parent may think that he or she is protecting the spouse and therefore is doing something "good" for the other. But this is no protection. It is usually better to get the truth out, then deal together with the feelings and the issues as they are shared openly with one another.

Whatever else, this is the child of *both* of them.

Brothers and sisters need to be told and most properly by the homosexual person, although it may be that the parents would be present for that session. The parents' presence may be expecially important if the siblings being told are middle teen age or younger. The homosexual son or daughter may, of course, want to tell older brothers and sisters without your being present. We believe that they have this right. Brothers and sisters will find out or be told eventually, so tell them now in a straightforward way at their particular level of understanding. We are aware, of course, that sometimes brothers and sisters who are adults move away from each other, have little communication, sometimes have intense conflict, and that there are circumstances in which a responsible choice is made not to inform them.

The same is true of grandparents, aunts, uncles, and cousins who are close, not only geographically but also in terms of genuine caring. How? "We have something that we have to tell you because we know that you love us and Marie. She has just told us she is homosexual. We're deeply disappointed and hurt and confused and angry. We feel bad about ourselves and are feeling guilty. But we love her and are trying to understand and work this through with each other. We need your support and prayers as we do so. Marie, of course, was anxious about telling us and is anxious about your knowing, but she also believed that it was important to our family life to be open and honest. She loves you, and although it may be difficult, wants to be able to talk with you about it the next time you see each other." Naturally, you would use the words that genuinely fit your experience and are applicable to your son or daughter. Also there are many times when it is more appropriate that your son or daughter write or talk to the relatives rather than your doing so.

There will, as we have suggested, occasionally be some exceptions to what we have been recommending here. Each homosexual person, along with the parents, will need to talk the matter over in detail and weigh the advantages and disadvantages.

Depending on circumstances, you may feel it important to tell some close friends, neighbors, the minister, people at the church, as you feel the need and as the occasion arises. The point to grow toward, and it certainly takes growth for quite a majority, is to be able to respond spontaneously in the middle of a conversation. When Joe says, "By the way, has old Bill gotten married yet?" you'll be able to reply: "No, Joe, he hasn't and he won't. Bill told us a few months ago that he was homosexual. It was a real blow to us and it left our heads spinning. We had to go through a lot with each other, but we're working it out. And that's just the way it is." Again, obviously, you use the words to describe yourself as you really are in this situation.

Once again, we want to remind you that you are not alone, and it is both unrealistic and hurtful to think and act as if you were. For every homosexual person there are parents, and they live around you, and some of them are already your friends. If some of you could identify one another, it would be natural and productive for you to share your experiences and band together in getting information that will guide your thinking and your feeling reactions. This could be done through informal conversations and with just a bit of planning effort. In addition, you and perhaps another couple or two might discuss the possibility of starting a somewhat larger group which would meet on a more regular basis for discussion and the gaining of information and become a chapter of Parents of Gays. (For information about this organization, write Betty Fairchild, Parents of Gays, 1435 Vine Street, Apt. 6, Denver, Colo. 80206.)

Within your church, as within most groups, there will probably be persons who understand and persons who don't. There will be those who will actively seek to support you and those who, in reacting to their own feelings of intense discomfort, will pull away.

There will be ministers who can be extremely helpful to you and some who will not be able to help. There are only two alternatives. One is to keep silent and fail to receive the personal sustenance you need. The other is to share the information and your experiences with fellow church members when it is appropriate to do so, realizing that some will be disconcerted and not know how to respond, but you will also be putting yourself in the position of receiving the helpful listening and expressions of love that you need from a number of others.

Finally, you are never "alone in the universe." In the midst of what is so often experienced as a terrible aloneness, feeling cut off from others whom until now you have thought you could count on, you may also feel deserted by God. If this is the case, even in this you are not alone. Jesus, and the psalmist before him (Ps. 22), cried out, "My God, my God, why hast thou forsaken me?" But the Bible makes clear that even though this is the way they *felt* at the time, God was still present with them and for them. God can assist you, too, in sustaining you as persons and as a family in the larger community in which you live as you struggle with your own feelings, your thoughts, and your relationships with one another.

8. What Is Homosexuality Anyway?

From what we have been saying up to this point, people's reactions to homosexuals and their attitudes about homosexuality seem to reflect a confusing vacillation between two strong emotional opinions. Somehow at one and the same time it is a dread social disease, which produces a sense of shame in the parents and which needs psychological treatment, and it is willfully and perversely chosen immorality, which the person could stop if only he or she wanted to, really loved the parents, accepted Christ, or whatever.

What is homosexuality and what causes it? Parents who are struggling with their own emotional reactions and their lack of understanding need help in trying to answer these questions for themselves in order to gain more meaningful perspective. Unfortunately, while the discussion presented in this chapter may assist parents in understanding their homosexual son or daughter better, it will not clear up all the confusion.

A great deal has been written and spoken about this subject, especially in the last fifteen years. A clear definition of the word "homosexual" which is acceptable to all has not been made and may not be. For the purposes of this book, however, homosexuality is defined as sexual attraction, emotional attachment, and/or sexual relations with someone of the same sex *over a period of time* in *adult* life. (See the discussion of a definition in Chapter 3.) This does not preclude sexual acts or emotional attachments or even marriage with a person of the opposite sex. Neither does it preclude a decision to remain celibate.

What is the cause of homosexuality? This is where it really gets complicated. There are three major theories that seek to answer this question. The first is a physical theory that proposes biological differences between homosexuals and heterosexuals. The differences studied have been for the most part in the areas of endocrinology and genetics. There has been and continues to be great interest in and research into the complexities of the physiology of human sexuality. One of the leading proponents of this view is Dr. John Money of the Johns Hopkins psychohormonal research unit. He has stated: "Researchers have not figured out as yet the formula whereby homosexual behavior patterns are, shall we say, built into the system. Present evidence strongly indicates both a prenatal and postnatal component to everybody's sexuality, whether homosexual, heterosexual, or bisexual." (Dr. John Money, "Differing Perspectives on Masters and Johnson," *Behavioral Medicine,* June 1979, p. 23.) However, there is presently no conclusive evidence that homosexuality is organically caused.

The second theory about the cause of homosexuality has to do with the environment of the family of origin of the homosexual person. There are many descriptions of the various family systems which seem to predispose to homosexuality. Most of these studies are based on data about families gleaned from the memories and experiences of homosexuals, usually of those who are troubled enough to be in psychotherapy. Through several decades of gathering information and carefully compiling many reports there seem to be some reappearing patterns.

1. A powerful mother figure who is both feared and needed and a father who is passive and ineffectual, often absent.

2. An overprotective mother who is possessive and controlling with a father figure who is controlled and withdrawn.

3. A hostile, aggressive, rejecting father with a seductive but sexually inhibited mother who needs the attention and dependence of her son for her own self-worth.

4. Both parents passive, overprotective, and afraid of aggression.

5. Both parents critical, demanding, aggressive, perfectionistic.

6. Consistent devaluation or idealization of either men or women generally, often by a single parent, either in an intact family or a divorced person.

7. Sibling rivalry in which one child is consistently dominated and his or her sexuality is devalued.

8. Seduction or erotic exploitation during childhood by an older sibling, parent, or other extended family member over a period of time. This can be the same or opposite sex family member.

9. An all-female-dominated environment with emasculating behavior. The entire locus of power in females is seen as possibly causative for both male and female homosexuals.

Irving Bieber studied two groups of a hundred men, one group homosexual, the other not. All two hundred men were in therapy. The key difference in family dynamics was that the father in the homosexual's family was emotionally detached and sometimes hostile to his son and was not "present" to aid his son in breaking away from the domination of his overinvolved, overprotective mother. Bieber says, "A constructive, supportive, warmly related father precludes the possibility of a homosexual son; he acts as a neutralizing protective agent should the mother make seductive close binding attempts." (Irving Bieber et al., *Homosexuality: A Psychoanalytic Study*, p. 162; Basic Books, 1962.)

This finding does *not* mean that the family system described invariably produces a homosexual son. If that were so, there would be many instances of all or more than one of the sons in a family being homosexual, and that is extremely rare. Every clinician works with men and women whose family dynamics are "classical" homosexual producers, but who are definitely heterosexual.

Conversely, there are many homosexual men and women who report not only adequate, but warm, loving, and well put together families. They tend to be persons who do not need to seek professional help. The trouble and pain of a variety of kinds experienced by homosexual persons whose family experiences were less than ideal are the forces that lead them to treatment. Being homosexual is often the least of their problems.

If your son or daughter has taken the initiative to tell you about his or her sexual orientation, it may be encouraging for you to note that the homosexual person who wants to reveal this to the parents is exhibiting some faith in you and in the family system. Whether that faith has any reality basis is tested in the ensuing process after the revelation.

If you have already been feeling guilty about your possible role in your son's or daughter's becoming homosexual, your feelings probably haven't been helped by this previous discussion. On the one hand, you may reject the implication that you are one of these "bad" families or persons and resent our having written what we have. On the other hand, you may be blaming yourself and/or your spouse even more, because you can think of this or that thing you have done "wrong." (See Chapter 5.) Let us say a couple of things. First, by listing particular sets of family relationships, we are not saying that parents are bad people. We are merely summarizing descriptions of families as they have been observed by researchers or perceived by the homosexual persons who have grown up in them. Even good, loving people have a variety of personal needs which lead them to relate in certain ways in their families, and these forms of relationships affect us all in these families in complex ways. This leads to the second point. To be involved with one another in a family, and then someone in the family be homosexual, alcoholic, mentally ill, or whatever, is not the same thing as stating that one parent or both parents have *caused* the condition. Human behavior is so complex that there cannot be a simple, direct causation. Other factors also play their roles. However, the way in which we seek to get our needs met by others within the family and the degree to which we do and do not meet one another's needs have their influence on our emotional life and our behavior, including our "outside the family" relationships.

The third major theoretical approach to the cause of homosexuality is developmental. This theory proposes that as a child develops from infancy into adulthood there are a multitude of events, both external and internal, physiological and psychological, which eventuate in a particular and unique self. Each child is born into a particular family, to a particular mother who is in a particular stage of her own adolescent or adult development, fathered by a male parent in his particular stage. This child is born at a particular season with his or her own particular pattern of genes which includes such critical items as sex, body shape and size, and neurological composition which includes perceptual potentials. This child is also born into a larger context of community and world in which specific events and conditions take place which can and do have critical impact on parents and therefore on the child as well. During the course of growth a child begins to make observations and come to conclusions about himself or herself and the world. The basic task for each child is to survive and then to feel comfortable and safe. Then the task is to grow and begin to be a separate person capable of caring for self. It sounds simple, but it isn't. As each child goes through this process there are conclusions reached which are perceived as the hard-and-fast rules of life. Sometimes rules are made which are distortions of reality as it now exists, but which were believed to be essential by the child when they were made.

A mother reports the following story. "My husband was overseas when our son was born. He was with me only two weeks after I found out I was pregnant. I stayed in the city where we'd been living because I had a job there and because there were so many memories. I moved in with another woman whose husband left when Jim did. I had an easy pregnancy, but I was anxious and sad a lot of the time because the war was so bad where he was. Sometimes I'd go weeks without hearing and then get a batch of letters. The baby came three weeks early, but he was okay. Little Jim was my joy and comfort. I talked to him like he was able to understand all the loneliness and fear I felt. I told that little baby long stories about his dad and how it was going to be when he got home. My girl friend worked a late shift, so I went back to work pretty soon and she was with him during the day. I got an older neighbor to take care of him for the two hours a day we couldn't cover. We three had a pretty good time, really, except for worries about our husbands' return.

"Little Jim was almost two when Jim came home. He had been wounded in one of the last battles in the South Pacific and although it wasn't bad, he had to be in the hospital for a while when he came back. Little Jim and I went every day and he could join us on the grounds. It was spring and I was so happy to have my husband back. I was happy, too, that he could at last see our baby. But somehow those two never did hit it off. Little Jim didn't want his daddy to hold him, and to tell the truth, I don't think Jim ever really wanted to hold his son. We had another little boy about a year after Jim got back. We had our own home. Jim was working and was with me all during my pregnancy. It really made a difference. Bobby is Jim's boy and Little Jim has always been all mine."

Here we have an example of the process in which larger events and particular family situations impact on the way one little boy perceived himself and his parents. It is also an example of how parents saw themselves and each other and their first child. The second son and his brother have some significant differences in the way they view and relate to their parents now. The boys are aware of themselves and are seen by others as quite different from each other.

Each of these boys went through specific and identifiable stages while growing up. These stages are identified with different terms by different theorists, but all theorists agree that there is nothing random about the progression from one developmental stage to the next. Sometimes because of a traumatic incident or because of a poorly functioning family system, a child may not go through a developmental stage successfully or completely. The child keeps right on growing and going through the rest of the stages, but a distortion is created which remains to be corrected.

Throughout the stages of development there is discovery and decision about one's body, including factors that influence sexual identity, how one views oneself as male or female, and how one relates to the same and the opposite sex. These stages are always a compound of internal and external stimuli. The child arrives at puberty with this sexual identity now being compounded by the hormonal storms of adolescence. Clear and strong sexual feelings arise. Body size and contours change rapidly during these adolescent years. By the end of adolescence sexual identity is set. There are many in the field who would put the age of clear sexual identity much earlier than this, although there is no agreement as to which age or in which stage of development.

Some attention needs to be paid to the work of Masters and Johnson with homosexuals at their laboratory/clinic in St. Louis (William H. Masters and Virginia Johnson, *Homosexuality in Perspective;* Little, Brown & Co., 1979). The basis for their treatment is the idea that sexuality, including specific forms of sexual expression, is learned. One learns to enjoy and repeat homosexual behavior and one learns to enjoy and repeat heterosexual behavior. In a sense we "learn" all our behavior, but this view is more complicated than it appears on the surface. Predisposition, instinct, or tendency to choose in one direction or the other is probably not random. But once a stimulus is experienced positively and is repeated with the same results, it becomes "learned." Awareness of the disadvantage of a particular behavior, in this case homosexual orientation, can lead to a decision to change the behavior. Masters and Johnson have reported a 65 percent "cure" rate for homosexuals who want to change and who have gone through an intensive two-week "unlearning" and "relearning" process.

There has been a controversy of some magnitude among professionals who research and treat problems of sexuality over Masters and Johnson's report. Some are critical of the research design and statistics. Some believe that although behavior was changed, fantasies and attitudes, and therefore many aspects of sexuality, remained the same. Masters and Johnson are to be commended, nevertheless, for continuing their investigations of human sexual functioning, this time homosexuality, an area that has been kept taboo for too long. Clearly, the debate will continue for some time around this issue. It is important to note that the more open the debate and the more interest shown, the more options are given to those who wish to understand their own sexuality. In addition, for those who want to change a homosexual orientation to a heterosexual one, the more methods of treatment the better.

Clearly no single cause and effect theory can explain homosexuality. We believe that it is not a single clinical entity. There are large numbers of variables which must come together in order for homosexuality to be the outcome. For the authors of this book, at this time a multifactor cause seems most plausible, and the set of influences that result in homosexuality in one person will differ from those which lead to this sexual orientation in another. The mystery of "Why?" and "How?" will remain veiled for some time, but with the removal of stigma and hatred and with added insights of continued research and treatment we can move forward to acceptance and reconciliation in the families of homosexuals.

9. But Doesn't the Bible Condemn Homosexuality?

For parents who are Christians, who belong to the church and for whom participation in the church has some real meaning, the question posed in this chapter title is pertinent. Although we parents are quite probably aware of our own sins and shortcomings, to the extent that we are deeply serious about our Christian commitment these sins are painful to us. Our response is properly to seek forgiveness and renewal of life in the Spirit, and move on. But homosexuality! It really seems different to us. It *feels* different when it is our own son or daughter who is involved, and regardless of what we say and do, he or she doesn't seem to change. It is as if this child who has been so dear to us now continues to live the life which we understand the Bible and Christian tradition to be condemning. A man we know literally groans with agony when he speaks of his son's living in constant sin and his seeming unwillingness to make a conscientious attempt to change. This is a deeply emotional issue for many parents, and we want to try to deal with it at that level of seriousness.

There is little question that the mainstream of Christian tradition over the centuries has been such as to make homosexuals feel either unwelcome or uncomfortable, or both, in the church. Only in very recent years have any Christian groups ordained into their ministry persons who were openly known as homosexual. With the exception of the Metropolitan Community Church, which is a growing association of congregations whose ministry is primarily directed to gays, such ordinations are still quite rare. Anyone who has been around, though, is aware that there are some homosexuals in the ministry of the mainline churches and that there always have been. They simply are not *known* to be gay. The ministry of these hidden homosexuals has been pretty much like that of heterosexuals: effective, ineffective, and in between, depending on the gifts and graces and willingness to work which they bring to it and not upon their sexual orientation.

Presumably this tradition against the inclusion of known homosexuals in the life of the community of faith has been based upon the "anti-homosexual" passages in the Bible. Some parents who are in the church (or even who have been in the past) use the Bible as a way of expressing their horror at and anger against their children. One mother almost immediately responded: "Haven't you read your Bible? Don't you know what it says?" However, what struck the son most about her reaction was that she had never taken the Bible that seriously before. Some parents insist that their children read the passages condemning homosexuality, as if somehow it would motivate them to change. It doesn't. Even when the homosexual is a sincere Christian person, by the time the person tells the parents, the biblical issue, the sin issue, has often been dealt with.

Since the Bible is certainly clear enough that heterosexuals can sin (and most of us have accumulated sufficient personal evidence to support that fact), then somehow homosexuality must have been viewed and continues to be viewed by a large number of Christians as somehow being a different order of sin. How could this be so? It seems to us that there is a great deal of confusion at this point. The Bible is not ambiguous on one issue: "All have sinned and fall short of the glory of God" (Rom. 3:23), and "none is righteous, no, not one" (3:10). The Bible knows no different order of sin, except perhaps the difficult reference by Jesus to an "unpardonable sin," but by no wildest stretch of the imagination can we draw out of that text that he is speaking of homosexuality. Therefore, homosexuality must be like other sin and yet *not* like other sin at the same time. Again, how can this be? We propose two responses: one is on an emotional level and the other on the level of how we go about trying to understand the Scripture.

First, let us ask you a question. Do you take *all* biblical injunctions with equal seriousness and emotional intensity? For example, are you part of a crusade to stop the crossbreeding of cattle or the planting of more than one crop in a single field? Do you refuse to wear clothing that is made of more than one kind of fiber? A ridiculous question! Yet these are definitely prohibited in Lev. 19:19, which is part of the same Holiness Code that had its origin in the sixth century B.C. and that also states, "You shall not lie with a male as with a woman" (18:22), which apparently was written to *men only*, the same prohibition also being made in 20:13.

Do you take all biblical injunctions with the same seriousness? Obviously not! Do you understand all the statements of this *whole* code (Lev. 17 to 26) to be equally applicable centuries later? Read all ten chapters, not only with reference to the several different things we have already mentioned but also with its guidelines for making burnt sacrifices, harvesting crops, how priests should dress and do their hair, and so forth. Obviously, none of us follows all of this to the letter. Do you even want to apply literally the two verses dealing with homosexuality? Probably not. In addition to the point already made, that is, apparently written to men only, both of the verses apply literally only to males. They do not explicitly prohibit lesbianism. (Does that now immediately change the way you *feel* about your *daughter's* situation?) The other fact is that Lev. 20:13 requires the death penalty for a male homosexual act. Even to the extent that your own feelings toward a son who is homosexual are extremely negative, do you believe deeply that the death penalty is called for?

There could be literally hundreds of illustrations that indicate to us that *none* of us takes all biblical commandments as having the same degree of relevance for our lives today and with the same intensity of emotional reaction. Why is this true? First, we have different sets of experiences that lead us into radically different emotional responses to different behaviors (for example, our experience with wearing cloth made of two fibers has usually been that it is really not such a big deal; we have never been threatened by it; it is not socially disruptive or personally harmful). Or, second, we have some principle of biblical interpretation that tells us that some biblical statements are not applicable to us *today* in *our* society as they were to the people of *that* day in *their* society, while other biblical statements are not only still relevant but authoritative.

In all honesty, it has been our experience that in the church our major emotional reaction against homosexuality is not primarily on the basis that the *Bible* condemns it, but that *we* as human beings condemn it. We condemn it because of what we have learned from our society, because of our misconceptions about homosexuals, who they are and what they do, and because from time to time either it has touched our lives or we have heard of it when it has touched the lives of others in ways that arouse our fear, revulsion, and anger. This is not to suggest that if only people had accurate information they would inevitably think that homosexuality was perfectly all right, but simply to state our conviction that the intensity of emotional reaction against homosexuality comes from a variety of social learning factors and from personal experiences rather than from the interpretation that the Bible says that it is wrong.

We have just read of a case where a man not far from us has been sentenced to prison because he fondled and exposed himself to small boys. Much public reaction labeled that as homosexuality. "That's what we have to fear!" Certainly there may be something to fear in this type of incident, but the man is not homosexual. He has another disorder. Or we read of a homosexual affair that ended in a jealous fight and murder. Of course that happens, but far less often than in heterosexual quarrels that also end in violent death. And on it goes.

We feel revulsion, fear, and anger. Then we *use* the Bible (or at least what we have *heard* about the Bible) to support *our* emotional reactions. As Christians, we can hardly condone any sin, but do we respond to all sin (sins), or *all* sinners, with the same emotional intensity? Most of us just do not, for example: the white-collar crimes (jockeying figures on books to someone's financial advantage), blue-collar crimes (just a few boards and pieces of pipe and a tool or two from the plant. "Thou shalt not steal," but the company is so big, so rich, they'll never miss it). Do we also get enraged about what the Bible seems to point to as the *central* sin, the one out of which all others come, idolatry, having *some* other god before Jehovah God. Let's isolate socially all people who bear false witness. Let's root them out of the church. Let's not ordain anyone who covets. *"All* have sinned and fall short of the glory of God," and the sin of many of us sinners is to view other sinners as far worse sinners than we, and so we condemn *them* and place restrictions on *them* in the church.

We have to deal with the Leviticus verses, of course. They command that the male homosexual act not take place. (Also notice that they do not command a man not to *be* homosexual or to have homosexual *feelings.*) In this sense, it is an *act* that these verses condemn. If, on the basis that the purpose of the entire Holiness Code is to clarify and to maintain the distinctive integrity of the

Hebrew people as the people of God in contrast with the other nations around them who worship other gods, we make the judgment that therefore the injunctions found in it are not necessarily applicable to many other people, Christian people, in different nations of the world today, how is it that we pay attention to some of these commands and none whatsoever to others? One way many Christians would respond to this is by suggesting that we test the older Jewish practices by New Testament standards and guidelines, the revelation of God in *Christ*. If this is one of our principles of biblical interpretation, then at least temporarily we have to leave the Leviticus verses aside until we look at the New Testament, and therefore these two verses cannot stand *by themselves* as being valid as a contemporary commandment anymore than the one that states, "If it [the peace offering sacrifice] is eaten at all on the third day, it is an abomination" (Lev. 19:7).

Before we go to the New Testament, however, we must take a trip to Sodom, since the events of one evening in that city have usually been called upon to bear some substantial weight of condemnation of homosexuality. However, if a person reads the story carefully, and also reads later references to Sodom in other books of the Bible, it is seen that homosexuality *as such* is not the main focus of attention in the description of the city as being so sinful that it should be destroyed. (There is a similar story in Judges 19, but not located in Sodom.) We shall give only a brief summary here, and for those who desire to read in more detail about Sodom or the whole issue of the Bible's dealing with homosexuality, we suggest that you read the excellent chapters in three other books, although they differ somewhat from one another in certain details of interpretation: Betty Fairchild and Nancy Hayward, *Now That You Know: What Every Parent Should Know About Homosexuality* (Harcourt Brace Jovanovich, 1979); Victor P. Furnish, *The Moral Teaching of Paul: Selected Issues* (Abingdon Press, 1979); Letha Scanzoni and Virginia Ramey Mollenkott, *Is the Homosexual My Neighbor? Another Christian View* (Harper & Row, 1978).

In the first place, it is quite clear in this story in Genesis 19 that the men of the city wanted to have sexual relationships with Lot's two guests, who were actually angels disguised as men. However, it was not merely that they *wanted* such relationships but also that they wanted Lot to hand his guests over to them against his and his guests' will. They threatened violence; they pushed forward as if to break into the house; they were intent on sexual aggression, literally rape. If this passage is used against homosexuality, then it must in all fairness be against homosexual *rape,* and could be used as appropriately against heterosexual rape as it could against *consenting* homosexual acts, the last *not* being an issue in this story at all. We well know today that any kind of rape is not the result of a strong sex drive, although a sexual act is involved, but it is primarily the result of hostility and aggression and is almost exclusively a *male* act. It is a form of personal violence.

Yet even as bad as their requests and threatening acts were, it was apparently not the main sin of the people in the city and not *the* reason God destroyed it. That decision had been made earlier. Judging on the basis of later passages that look back upon the city at that time, the reasons were more widespread: "Behold, this was the guilt of . . . Sodom: she and her daughters had pride, surfeit of food, and prosperous ease, but did not aid the poor and needy. They were haughty, and did abominable things before me" (Ezek. 16: 49–50). Although the writer of Ezekiel might well have had in mind the night of threatened sexual aggression when he spoke of "abominable things," he does not make any specific reference to homosexuality at all. He *does* come down hard on those who have much of the world's goods, who are proud of it, and who do not out of their abundance aid the poor and needy. Where does *that* leave many of *us* in the eyes of God? Just to emphasize the point, we mention that farther on in Ezekiel (in ch. 22), there is a listing of the sins of the people at the time of the writing of the book of Leviticus itself, among which are several sexual ones (22:10–12), but homosexuality is *not* among them.

Of the nine New Testament references to Sodom, not one mentions homosexuality specifically. Jude, verse 7, does say that the people of the city acted "immorally." The Greek word here refers to sexual immorality in general. The verse goes on to add that they "indulged in unnatural lust," literally, "went after other flesh," which might refer to homosexuality or, as some scholars suggest, the desire to have sexual relations with angels (Furnish, *The Moral Teaching of Paul,* p. 56). Second Peter 2:7 refers to the "licentiousness of the wicked," again the word translated "licentiousness" referring to sexual immorality in general. The other New Testament references to Sodom (Matt. 10:15 and its parallel, Luke 10:12; Matt. 11:23–24; Luke 17:29; Rom. 9:29; and Rev. 11:8) say nothing at all about homosexuality or any specific sin. They are all used as illustrations of the certainty of God's judgment on cities where people did not receive God's messengers.

Finally, those who read the King James Version may see several places where the word "sodomite" is used. In every instance, according to Dr. Furnish, "the reference is to male prostitutes associated with places of worship" (*The Moral Teaching of Paul*, p. 57), and therefore not to homosexuality as a condition nor to homosexual relationships in the usual sense. In the Old Testament the attacks against the male *and female* temple prostitutes are not on the basis that they engaged in sexual acts, but that the acts reflected their worship of other gods (pp. 57–58).

The total impact of all of this is that the story of Sodom is a very poor one, indeed a quite inappropriate one, to use as a condemnation of homosexuality as a condition (it says absolutely nothing about that) or of homosexual acts between consenting persons (it doesn't say anything at all about that, either). It *can* be used to oppose homosexual desire that is linked with aggression. And, of course, if we are to use the Ezekiel verses, the entire story of Sodom can very well be used to condemn complacent luxury and neglect of the poor and needy, which is a frequent and persistent theme throughout the entire Old and New Testament, with literally scores of references, in stark contrast with the Bible's *very* rare statements about homosexual acts.

At this point, then, we have discovered only four references in the entire Old Testament: the two in the Leviticus passage (literally male with male, with the death penalty required, and with the whole Holiness Code now awaiting our examination of the New Testament in order to determine what is and is not valid for us today), the story in Judges, and the story of Sodom, in the midst of which is a horrible scene in which men wanted to force sex on two angels disguised as men, by violence if necessary. It certainly seems quite fair to say that the Old Testament has very little concern with homosexual acts except as these may reflect the worship of alien gods or when they are in the context of aggression. Very obviously adultery is seen as far more destructive to family and larger social life, since both the act of adultery and even *coveting* a neighbor's wife are a part of the Ten Commandments and homosexual acts are not.

When we look at the New Testament we are once again struck by the fact that it is rather difficult to find any statements about homosexuality. *Jesus never mentions it at all.* He was hardly one to let serious sin go by unnoticed and unmentioned. Of course, Jesus didn't waste time cataloging sins and giving complete lists of them to a scribe to write down. He responded to specific situations with which he was confronted. Therefore, either homosexuality never became an issue at all to him, or if it came up, the early church didn't think it that important when it came to recording what was essential for their church life and faith.

In addition to the brief reference to Sodom in Jude, where the meaning might be applied to homosexual lust, which we have already discussed, there are only three other verses in the entire New Testament. In commenting briefly upon these, we are following Dr. Furnish's exegesis very closely, since his conclusions seem to be more soundly based on the original language in its larger cultural and biblical context than any other we are familiar with.

Before Furnish discusses the passages themselves, he goes into some detail about homosexual practices in the first-century Mediterranean world in order to arrive at and document three essential points that make up a rather common understanding of the meaning of homosexual acts in that day. "First, not only the terms, but also the concepts 'homosexual' and 'homosexuality' were unknown in Paul's day. These terms, like the terms 'heterosexual,' 'heterosexuality,' bisexual,' and 'bisexuality,' presume an understanding of human sexuality that was possible only with the advent of modern psychological and sociological analysis. The ancient writers . . . were operating without the vaguest conception of what we have learned to call 'sexual orientation.' " (Furnish, *The Moral Teaching of Paul*, pp. 65–66.)

The distinction that we make today between a person's psychological and/or physiological *condition* of being and the acts that a person performs simply was not a possibility in their manner of thinking.

Therefore, second, merely an elaboration of the first point, a homosexual act was understood to be a perverse extension of heterosexual desire, that which happens when heterosexual lust is so great that it is not adequately fulfilled by someone of the opposite sex. It was an act that was the reflection of a person's excessive lust, lack of willpower, and, of course, for Jews and Christians, therefore of ungodliness.

Finally, the first-century non-Christian writers about homosexual behavior saw it as necessarily involving one person's exploitation of another: subjects by rulers, slaves by masters, young boys by older men. Even when there were two consenting adults, homosexual acts were understood as robbing the submissive partner of his maleness (remember, everything was written *by* males primarily *to* males and *usually* about male behavior) and was therefore literally still an exploitation, a robbing.

The *condition* of homosexuality as an exclusive or primary sexual orientation, established very or relatively early in life by whatever means, leading to a relationship of love, respect, intimacy, and commitment with another of similar *condition* was not a part of their understanding or thinking or experience at all.

Given this social context and way of viewing behavior, it is not difficult to see that such practices would fall short of the standard of obedience and service to the God whose compassion and valuing of persons were made concrete and clear in Jesus. Christians would not be *driven* by lust, would not exploit others, would not rob them of vital aspects of their personhood. With this being so obvious, let's look at the specific texts.

First Corinthians 6:9, while clear to some is not clear to others. Just a look at a half dozen or so of the different versions of the Bible shows the difficulty that scholars themselves have in trying to determine the English words that might most accurately convey Paul's intent when he wrote in Greek. Even though the Revised Standard Version, *The Jerusalem Bible*, and *The New English Bible*, to mention a few, all use words like "homosexuals" or "homosexual perverts," the original Greek has two distinct words. The first means "soft" or "weak," which leads to the King James Version's use of the word "effeminate." The use of this Greek word in nonbiblical writings of that time suggests that it could be used for the passive partner in a male homosexual relationship, and Paul could well be using it in this way. The second word means something like "males who go to bed," and when used in combination with the first word could mean the sexual partner who assumes the traditional active role. Furnish's own translation reads: "men who assume the feminine role in sex, nor men who have sex with them" (Furnish, *The Moral Teaching of Paul*, p. 70). This, of course, means that the statement probably does have to do with male homosexual acts. These words are found in a list that is representative of (not comprehensive and complete, but *representative* of) the behaviors of people who *belong* to this world, who are ungodly, who have not been "set apart for God's service, affirmed as righteous," and who "will not get into God's Kingdom" (Furnish's translation).

When we realize the meaning that sexual acts between males had for people of that day (insatiable lust, exploitative, often temple prostitution and therefore indicative of the worship of other gods, in many other instances coercive in the sense of taking advantage of someone with less social and/or personal power), it is clear that these acts cannot describe someone who is responding to God's loving call to enter into the Kingdom. It is also important to notice some *other* examples in this same list of those who will not enter the Kingdom: idolaters, adulterers, drunkards, money-grabbers (the "greedy," RSV), slanderers. There is no indication that one of these examples of unrighteousness is more or less serious than another. They simply present a range of behaviors that would not be descriptive of someone who *is* going to enter the Kingdom.

The list in I Tim. 1:9–10 is similar in intent, that is, to suggest a range of behaviors, not to be an exhaustive cataloging of persons who, in the context in this letter, are those for whom God's law is designed, the "lawless and disobedient." One of the words used in this passage is the second of the two words referred to in I Cor. 6:9, "men who [actively] have sex with other men." Also included in the Timothy list are the "profane, . . . liars, perjurers."

These two lists (I Corinthians and I Timothy) state *some* of the behaviors that are displeasing to God and that are symptomatic of sin. Homosexual behavior *as it was understood at that time* was displeasing to God.

The major passage in the Bible as far as sounding condemnatory of homosexuality is concerned is Rom. 1:26–27. It is also the one and only scriptural reference to homosexual relations between females. This section as a whole (Rom. 1:18 to 3:20) has a theological purpose that is to proclaim that we are all in need of the grace of God. Paul proceeds by first showing in 1:18–32 the wickedness of the Gentiles, and he does so in terms that are characteristic of a number of Jewish critics of the Gentile world at that time. The theme is that because they have not recognized God as their creator through the "natural" means around them (nature and the general moral order), they have been "given up by God" to all kinds of wickedness. The base *sin* is not homosexuality nor any of the other behaviors listed; rather, it is not worshiping the true and living God. The results of not worshiping God are these kinds of behaviors, all of which are seen as conscious and willful. In other words, because they do not recognize the God that Christians now know in Christ, God has abandoned them to their various lusts, one of which is sexual, with homosexuality being one of these, and again, as we explained before, it being a conscious decision to act out one's unrestrained passion in this way rather than heterosexually within marriage. If we could assume that this is *what* homosexuality is, and *all* that it is, it could be seen as being in conflict with the behavior of one who does worship the living God.

To complete Paul's point, after he has described the Gentiles in this way, he hits the Jews: "You are no better. All have sinned. None can be justified on the basis of good works. We all can live only through the gracious forgiving acceptance of God as God is known through Jesus the Christ."

A summary of the logic of the New Testament position seems to be that if one denies the one God who is the creator and redeemer, one is vulnerable to domination by one's own lusts and passions, one's own persistent self-seeking. So far, so good. But insatiable sexual lust, so Paul and his contemporaries believed, leads on beyond heterosexual activity to the choice of someone of one's own sex as a partner in a way that inevitably involves exploitation. The best psychological investigations today do not uphold this view of the nature of the *homosexual person*, nor is that view descriptive of all homosexual acts, although obviously they *may* be lustful and exploitative, just as heterosexual expressions *may* be.

Now, what is the meaning for *us* of the two statements from Leviticus that we left hanging? It would seem that they and the New Testament, with Paul's addition of female homosexual acts but without the commandment concerning the death penalty, are saying about the same thing on this matter. If we fit all the biblical references together, a summary of the scriptural position on homosexuality would seem to be that the Bible has *no explicit position at all* on homosexuality as a condition. This is something which they knew nothing about and therefore could not have commented on. It is, however, a condition that we today know exists. Like other conditions and many modern situations about which the Bible does not speak, we are left with the necessity of seeking God's will in ways different from that of finding specific biblical statements of approval or disapproval. Where homosexual *acts* today are reflective of a disregard for the worship of God, where they are motivated only by the desire to fulfill one's own passion and are therefore selfish, where they are coercive and exploitative, then these fit the biblical descriptions of acts that are displeasing to God.

However, when persons are homosexual, this being a condition of persistent sexual preference, established early in life and/or having developed over a long period of time, and when two homosexual persons are in love with each other, respect and appreciate each other, commit themselves to the well-being of each other, and desire sexual relationships with each other, we are left with a situation untouched by the biblical descriptions and injunctions. These persons, who may also desire to serve God, must seek God's will for themselves on the basis of the impact of the total message of the gospel as it is found in Scripture, through prayer, and if possible, through discussion with other persons of faith.

We have pointed out that there are few references to homosexual acts in the Bible. These acts were understood in the very limited ways that we have tried to explain. They were understood as lustful, exploitative acts involving the rejection of God. Therefore, they are not applicable to the *condition* of homosexuality as we know it today. Yet, all of this is not the same thing as declaring that therefore the Bible says that homosexuality is okay, or that it is as much God's will as the heterosexual orientation that leads to marriage. To us, at least, the total impact of Scripture is on the side of God's plan for human beings involving heterosexual attraction and leading to a permanent marriage in which there is sexual fidelity. The Jewish emphasis on the bearing of children would rather clearly favor this position and would oppose homosexual relationships as a life-style of equal value. This seems to us to be the Scripture's portrayal of the primary will of God. It is what is expected. The exceptions to this in the Scripture are when a person in response to God's call to a particular mission in the world does not marry as a part of his effective carrying out of that mission (Jesus, Paul, others). However, when the condition or situation is such that the primary will of God is not possible for a person, and there are many such dilemmas in human life, the person of faith is not released from the obligation to seek what is *now* God's will for himself or herself from this time forward in the new situation. This seems to be the situation of many homosexual persons today. Their *being* homosexual does not call for condemnation from us. The *Bible does not* condemn their condition. If they are serious about being Christian, they seek God's will for themselves given the realities of their condition, and this is between them and God.

We believe that it is important for parents to distinguish between their own *personal* negative feelings toward the homosexuality of their son or daughter (lack of understanding, revulsion, anger, disapproval, even condemnation) and what the Bible actually does and does not say. We do not believe that the Bible, carefully and prayerfully read, is the source of the reaction of panic and dread and attack on homosexual persons. These strong negative reactions are parents' own personal ones, for their own personal reasons: the breakdown of their perception of reality concerning their son or daughter, their fear of what this means for the way they have lived their lives as parents, the changing of their expected future, their fear of social disapproval.

The impact of this chapter, as we understand it, is that a harsh condemnation of homosexuality is not supported by the Bible, nor does the Scripture place any particular focus on it as one of the "major sins." Our intent, however, is not to try to convince parents that the Bible approves of the homosexual condition (since it doesn't mention it), nor of homosexual acts (since the acts as *they* understood them *are* condemned). Reasonable and sincere Christian people may still, on the basis of the Bible, of what they might refer to as the "natural order of things," or for certain social reasons see homosexuality as opposed to God's primary will, a condition that was not intended in creation. These persons, therefore, would take the point of view that it is appropriate for the church to refuse to support any of the possible influences that might lead to homosexuality and that the church should not support homosexual behavior as a "viable alternative life-style," an expression we hear from time to time. This position, of course, would also include on the part of

Christians the attempt to understand homosexual persons and would certainly entail caring for them as we would any other person who is our "neighbor."

In the midst of the Bible's quite rare disapproval of certain kinds of homosexual acts (and many kinds of heterosexual acts), its silence about homosexuality as a condition and about loving and committed homosexual relationships, there is still the strong voice coming through loud and clear: "Judge not, that you be not judged. For with the judgment you pronounce you will be judged" (Matt. 7: 1–2).

But even behind that warning is the compassionate God who was the source of the life of Jesus and the source of our own life and the lives of our children. When God's love for us and our children is known, then the power for change in our attitudes and feelings and the power for reconciliation within our families begins to be effective: "Beloved, let us love one another; for love is of God, and he who loves is born of God and knows God. . . . We love, because he first loved us" (I John 4:7, 19).

10. What Does Our Child Want of Us?

We were sitting around the table having a lively and serious conversation with two gay men, one in his late twenties, the other in his thirties. They were interested in sharing with us details of their lives, past and present, which were significant to them. The younger had been describing the separation from his parents that he had felt early in his life. Well he might! He had been sent to a private school a great distance from his home from the very beginning. He saw his parents only once or twice a year. But it was emotional distance as well. As he grew older, along with his increasing recognition that he was gay, he also was aware of the resentment that he had toward them. His father was highly authoritarian, and they had great difficulty talking. After this young man became an adult and was completely into the gay life, with a great deal of fear he told his parents about his sexual orientation.

One of the authors of this book interrupted to ask the question which we, of course, are extremely interested in: "What was the reason you told them? After all you've told us about their sending you away for most of your childhood and teen age, your resentment about this, some of the other ways they treated you, were you interested in developing a better relationship with them?" The young man looked very surprised at this question, and the tone of his voice seemed to suggest that such a question was entirely un-necessary: "Of course!" "Of course" almost all children, of what-ever age, if they don't have it already, long for a good relationship with their parents. Regardless of what has and has not gone on between them, it is impossible for children, whether they are four, fourteen, twenty-four, or forty-four, to escape the reality that they are children of their own parents, emotionally bound and emotion-ally reactive to them. Of course, under some circumstances, teenage and adult children may need to put a distance between themselves and their parents: get away physically or change the nature of the emotional ties. It is also true, to be sure, that there are occasions when the relationship is so frustrating, so angering over a long period of time that a young man or woman will finally give up. "I don't care what they [the parents] think or how they feel anymore. I've had it!" This unfortunately can and does occasionally happen. But almost always there is the yearning for a relationship of mutual honesty, respect, friendship, an ease of being together in which a person can be himself or herself and be loved and accepted, a full and genuine member of the family.

"Of course!" even, or perhaps especially, when there's been es-trangement. There often has been a growing separation when the young person is gay. Sometimes the separation is open: there is constant anger and conflict, arguments, unpleasantness, or an obvi-ously cool distance. But very often it's not this at all. Rather, there is a gradually growing sense of discomfort. If the son or daughter has already left home, is at college or is working, the visits back begin to decrease in an effort to protect the parents. Being with them and continuing to pretend or at least allowing the parents to continue to think that their son or daughter is someone he or she is not; telling about friends, but being very careful not to tell too much about certain ones; about activities, but in a guarded way; about one's roommate, but—this feels like very dangerous ground. All of this caution, guardedness, defensiveness, occasional lying, leads to a great deal of anxiety and tension. It is difficult to have good, free-flowing conversations. It takes the fun out of the visit. It stands in the way of the developing adult-to-adult relationship which can be so satisfying for parents and their mature children. Therefore, there are fewer and shorter visits back home.

The son or daughter discourages visits from the parents. What would the son or daughter do to entertain the parents? Invite friends over? Go out to a favorite bar? Attend the Metropolitan Community Church on Sunday morning? And, if one is living with a lover, what does one do? Send the lover away? Spend several days trying to pretend that they're "just friends"? It is tense, awkward, artificial. It is a lie, and there is guilt about that.

If there is a particular lover in the picture, if there is a developing and committed relationship, it is only natural that they want to do more and more things together, just as young people want to do in a heterosexual relationship. It is natural to want to take a loved person home, introduce the person to one's parents, share the meaningful relationship with them. This is especially true at the time of holidays that have traditionally been family affairs: Thanksgiving, Christmas, one's own or a parent's birthday, others.

A man in his late thirties, a college teacher, formerly married and with children, "came out" a few years ago. In a talk he gave to a group of college counselors and administrators he said, "The most difficult thing about being homosexual is one's relationship to one's parents and other family members." Many young people who have been struggling with their own sexual identity over the years, who have been troubled by their strong feelings of attraction to persons of the same sex, who from time to time have had homosexual experiences, have felt very isolated and alienated from their own families, from their churches, from many of their lifelong friends, from society as a whole. They have had to struggle and work alone to try to make sense out of their own being. It has been agonizing and lonely and they haven't always known whom they could trust. Deep within themselves they have realized that being loved, accepted, and supported by members of their own families, especially their parents, is central in their coming to terms with themselves, breaking down the walls of isolation, gaining a sense of well-being and constructive direction for their lives. They are fearful for themselves and their parents when they think about opening up this issue for discussion. They plan, and don't initiate the conversation. This is repeated many times. They rehearse the words and imagine the reactions. These reactions range from the best ("You're our child and we love you. You can always be yourself with us") to the worst (weeping, fainting, denunciation, banishment). In their minds they swing from what they desire so passionately to their most fearful predictions.

Some never get around to initiating such a conversation, leaving the parents to discover the truth in some other way or live with unspoken suspicion or perhaps never knowing. Some finally take the plunge, fear and all. According to a young friend of ours who took an informal survey of her friends for us, only 11 percent had told their parents, 27 percent of the parents had found out in some other way, and to the young people's direct knowledge, 61 percent of the parents had neither been told nor found out in any other way. When we have talked with homosexual persons about their desires, with rare exceptions they would like to be able to talk about their sexual orientation openly with their parents and still be loved and accepted as their parents' child and as a genuine member of the family in every respect. Their great conflict is whether they can have the better relationship by telling or not telling. Either route is extremely difficult and has its particular tensions. But almost universally, they would like to have a good relationship with their parents, even though a few have reached the point of believing that such a goal is unattainable and they have given up, as we have said earlier.

What do these teenagers, these young adults really want? They want some different things, of course. Some might want their parents to direct them to a helpful professional or to someone who can help them figure themselves out. They want to know whether they are homosexual or not. Some are reasonably sure that they are, or are headed that way, and genuinely want to see if they can become heterosexual. Some may definitely be gay and do *not* want to change their sexual orientation. But even they would often like help in understanding themselves. Some who are promiscuous are thoroughly disgusted with that way of relating sexually and, while remaining gay, would like help in learning how to give up their present style of making sexual contacts and begin to establish long-lasting, meaningful relationships with a sexual partner.

But numerous homosexual persons do not feel themselves to be in need of the type of help we have been describing. With both groups, however, there is usually a common desire to have the type of relationship with their parents that a child of any age would want to have, and in so many instances, this calls for reconciliation. As Christians, "God, . . . through Christ reconciled us to himself *and gave us the ministry of reconciliation*" (II Cor. 5:18).

They would like, first of all, to feel that they can be honest with their parents, including, but not limited to, honesty about their own homosexuality. Such honesty presupposes that regardless of what parents hear from their sons or daughters, they will first attempt to understand what their children's experiences are like to them. Assuming that most parents have many of the thoughts and feelings that we have described in earlier chapters, these feelings need not block them from the necessary task which is the first step in maintaining any good relationship as well as being the first step in reconciliation, the attempt to *understand* the other.

Secondly, the homosexual son or daughter wants to be accepted for who he or she is. Not many teenagers and adults are so unrealistic as to expect that their parents will *approve* all of their behavior. After all, they don't approve of all of their parents' behavior either, nor even all of their own. But any one of us as human beings does not want to be wholly judged as a person on the basis of only one aspect of our lives. Time and again we have heard homosexual persons say something like: "I want them to look at me as who I am totally, not just at my sexual preference. After all, I'm the same person now as I was before they knew about this."

Our sons or daughters, homosexual *and* heterosexual, may be doing things in ways quite different from the ways we do them, may be doing things that we truly believe are wrong, may not be fulfilling their potential, may even be in serious trouble. We are pained and sometimes angered by this. But also, the son or daughter who is homosexual, even if we don't understand or approve of that, may also in other respects be living a very responsible life, have high moral standards, be loving and sensitive, have a deep and meaningful Christian faith. Even if we are deeply distressed by their *homosexuality*, they want us to see them as the *whole* persons they are.

Thirdly, as we have said before, they want to be as much members of the family in their own parents' eyes as anyone else is, as much as the child who met all your expectations, as much as their brothers and sisters who have gotten married and had children.

Parents usually find themselves in the midst of a crisis in the literal sense of the word when they discover that a son or daughter is homosexual. Their self-images, their images of the family, their reputation, the family system as a system is threatened. One way of attempting to deal with a crisis is to deny the reality of what has taken place and to behave, relate, and communicate rigidly in the ways they have done before. This strategy can work only to the detriment of the total family. Spontaneous loving relationships are transformed into anxious and strained pretense. This is not at all to say that the people cease to love. However, the openness and warmth is covered and bound by strained behavior, and beneath it all is great pain and a longing for reconciliation.

Another way of dealing with a crisis requires our feeling the pain and allowing it to be the stimulus that forces us to reexamine ourselves as individuals and as a family system, allowing the crisis to crack us open to be the *human* selves that we are, vulnerable to one another, yet trusting one another's responses. The crisis has the potential of pushing us to a level of informational exchange, awareness of our feelings, and the communication of our feelings that perhaps we have never had before and that would lead us into a new quality of loving relationship with one another. This is something else which your homosexual son or daughter probably wants of you and of themselves in relationship to you.

The crisis precipitated by the discovery that your son or daughter is homosexual may provide you and your family, in the midst of your disappointment and anger and confusion and pain and sadness, the opportunity for constructive change. The Bible does not offer to those who respond to God's love for them protection from a painful and even dangerous crisis. It does promise that nothing "will be able to separate us from the love of God in Christ Jesus our Lord," and it affirms that "we know that in everything God works for good with those who love him" (Rom. 8:39, 28).

The discovery that your son or daughter is homosexual may actually be a crisis of faith itself. The inevitable question of "Why?" arises spontaneously in the minds and on the lips of many. "Why me, Lord? Why that person? Why us? Why are you punishing us this way? How could you be all-loving and all-powerful and let something like this happen?" Natural cries of anger and anguish like these may lead to anger with God, denial of God, unrelieved guilt even after many prayers for forgiveness, a lessening of the meaning of participation in the community of faith, the church, even withdrawal from the church. It is possible for us to give ourselves over to these feelings and our faith diminishes, becomes less meaningful, and our whole life becomes limited in ways it was not limited before. Unfortunately, some people allow themselves to continue to live at that level. However, such a crisis and its feelings and questions can drive persons to a reexamination of the basics of faith, a more studied reading and discussion of the Bible, and an honest look at themselves in relationship to God in the light of what they are now in the process of discovering.

In reading the Bible, you have the possibility of sharing somewhat the same conclusion that we have come to and that we have elaborated upon in Chapter 9. While this view of the Bible's dealing with the issue of homosexuality may not change your immediate personal feelings, we hope that it might have the effect of providing the perspective which can facilitate your grappling with your feelings and working lovingly and constructively within your partly old, partly new relationship with your child.

On the other hand, you, along with other conscientious people, as a result of your inevitable conditioning in our society, as a result of your best understanding of the Scripture which then comes out at a position different from ours, or from reasoning on the basis of what you understand to be natural, or God's design in creation, may never come to the place where you can approve of homosexual acts. You genuinely believe them to be morally wrong.

If this is where you are, and if this is where you come out even as a result of a process of study and discussion, then you are faced with the task of reconciling your beliefs with the relationship which you truly want to have with your own son or daughter. Few people are willing to give up a relationship with their children in the name of faith. Your difficult task is to make a clear distinction between that behavior which you believe to be morally wrong, or sin, and your son or daughter, who from your point of view, is a sinner, *but still your child.* There is no faith position that allows us to control the behavior of another person, no matter how strongly we may personally wish it to be otherwise. But regardless of the choices of our own children, and they *will* make them about their own lives, we also want to experience the two-way communication of love in our relationships with them. In fact, we believe that faith itself includes within it the imperative to move toward developing a loving relationship between parent and child.

Therefore, no matter what your sincere belief is about what the Bible says concerning homosexuality and regardless of whether you believe it to be a sin or not, we believe that your awareness of the whole thrust of the biblical message and your continuing attempt to understand what it is saying to you in your situation at this time will lead you to understand that God *is,* God is *love,* God's love is *powerful,* and that God never stops seeking us or working with us to bring about our reconciliation to God and to one another. The lives of our children of whatever age are in God's hands. God is the one who offers to us all in whatever circumstances a new tomorrow.

In the midst of your present experience, whatever questions, thoughts, and feelings you might have, however the relationships in your family might be at this moment, it is possible to share the faith of the apostle Paul: "We are afflicted in every way, but not crushed; perplexed, but not driven to despair; persecuted, but not forsaken; struck down, but not destroyed. . . . For while we live we are always being given up to death for Jesus' sake, so that the life of Jesus may be manifested in our mortal flesh. . . . So we do not lose heart" (II Cor. 4:8–9, 11, 16).

Numerous parents have allowed their genuine love for and commitment to their son or daughter to sustain them in the demanding process of working through all that reconciliation entails. It is often a long process, lasting from many months to sometimes a few years. It involves allowing themselves to feel and express their strong and conflicting emotions. It means negotiating and renegotiating the tensions within the family. This refers to numerous discussions and often enough even arguments with the homosexual young person or adult and bearing periods of emotional and sometimes physical distancing. The successful resolution of the process necessitates getting through to the other side of the numerous occasions of wanting to give up. This process may also have included the questioning of God, the uneasiness with members of the church congregation, feeling a loss of faith. But the love and commitment to the son or daughter has prevailed, and faith has still operated to guide and sustain even periods when only its absence was felt.

In the final analysis, these parents did "not lose heart." Their reward has been the quality of relationship with their son or daughter that all parents and all children of whatever age long for: mutual love and respect and friendship and a sense of belonging. Numerous parents and their homosexual sons and daughters have reported such reconciliation. It is worth working for.

"Beloved, I am writing you no new commandment, but an old commandment which you had from the beginning.   And this commandment we have from him, that he who loves God should love his brother [sister, son, daughter, neighbor] also" (I John 2:7; 4:21).

For Further Reading

The following list includes books that are specifically written for parents and family members, some that are written with church members in mind, and some that are introductory in purpose. It is a very brief and selective list. We have deliberately omitted many excellent longer and more technical books and books dealing with the psychotherapy of homosexual persons. In addition, we must surely apologize to a number of authors for not including their books, which might very appropriately be listed here but were not simply because we were not aware of them. Attempting to become familiar with the entire literature of this field would have been an impossible task in the time allotted.

As you read two or three of the books on this list and begin to move through some of the emotional and relational stages that we have discussed in this book, we believe that it would make sense for you to consider reading some of the longer and more technical books. We suggest that you consult the bibliographies in the books below or in the books that we have mentioned in the text.

We also believe that for most parents there is little value in reading books that describe in detail the "gay life-style." Therefore, none of them is recommended *at this time*.

Arthur, L. Robert. *Homosexuality in the Light of Biblical Language and Culture: An Evangelical Approach.* Universal Fellowship Press, 1977.

A ten-page booklet by a minister of the Metropolitan Community Church, a specialist in biblical languages, who claims to "believe in the inspiration, inerrancy and literal interpretation of the scriptures" (p. 3). He nevertheless utilizes interpretative procedures of contemporary biblical criticism. His position is that the Bible does not condemn homosexual love or the homosexual condition.

Drakeford, John W. *A Christian View of Homosexuality.* Broadman Press, 1977.

A compassionate personal approach by a Southern Baptist professor of pastoral care. It comes down on an interpretation of the Bible that condemns homosexuality as such. This book recommends conversion.

Fairchild, Betty, and Hayward, Nancy. *Now That You Know: What Every Parent Should Know About Homosexuality.* Harcourt Brace Jovanovich, 1979.

A longer more detailed book that is probably the very next book a parent should read. There is sound, although not undisputed, information about homosexuality as a condition and a study of the relevant biblical passages and the positions of a number of churches on the issue of homosexuality. There is a great deal of case material. The book is easily read and very helpful.

Field, David. *The Homosexual Way: A Christian Option?* Inter-Varsity Press, 1979.

Very good scholarship by a British writer, who sets forth an "in-between" position on biblical interpretation. This book advocates abstinence for homosexuals as the biblical position.

Furnish, Victor P. *The Moral Teaching of Paul: Selected Issues.* Abingdon Press, 1979. Chapter 3, "Homosexuality."

The best single brief piece of writing we have seen on a biblical view of homosexuality. The position is drawn out at some length in our Chapter 9, but Furnish's entire chapter is worth reading.

Jones, Clinton R. *Understanding Gay Relatives and Friends.* Seabury Press, 1978.

A compassionate Christian approach to homosexual persons. This book is helpful in leading to increased understanding by relatives and friends.

Scanzoni, Letha, and Mollenkott, Virginia Ramey. *Is the Homosexual My Neighbor? Another Christian View.* Harper & Row, 1978.

A must for the Christian. Written by committed Christian persons, this book discusses the variety of issues surrounding homosexuals and homosexuality: the social setting, society's reactions, some of the knowledge we have about homosexuality, a chapter on the Bible, the response of churches, a "homosexual Christian ethic." Every book on this topic has debatable material and this one does also, but it is easily read, is competently done, and is important. There is an excellent bibliography.

Silverstein, Charles. *A Family Matter: A Parent's Guide to Homosexuality*. McGraw-Hill Book Co., 1977.

This book, written by a psychotherapist, was first recommended to us by several gay persons themselves who found it an excellent description of themselves, their self-image, their struggles, their relationships with their parents. It is competently done and generally helpful. However, we *do not* recommend that this book be the second or third book you read. We believe that many of our readers will be hindered in their own process of resolving their conflicted feelings by one emotionally charged chapter. However, after some further reading and after work on yourself and between husband and wife and discussions with your teenage or adult child, we believe that there are important insights to be gained from Silverstein.